PERSEVERING **T**HROUGH **S**EASONS OF **D**ESPAIR

A DAILY DEVOTIONAL BY DEBRA FREDETTE

EDITED BY ELEONOR GARDNER

I pray this book blesses you!

Debra Fredette

Scripture quotations marked NIV are taken from the Holy Bible, New International Version ®, NIV ® Copyright © 1973, 1978, 1984, 2011 by Biblica, Inc. Used with permission. All rights reserved worldwide. Scripture quotations marked (NLT) are taken from the Holy Bible, New Living Translation, copyright ©1996, 2004, 2015 by Tyndale House Foundation. Used by permission of Tyndale House Publishers, Carol Stream, Illinois 60188. All rights reserved.

Briley & Baxter Publications | Plymouth, Massachusetts

ISBN: 978-1-961978-05-8

Book Design: Stacy Padula

This book is dedicated with love and gratitude to all the men and women who have served and are currently serving in the United States Armed Forces, especially those in my immediate family:

WALTER IVAN — Army, World War I
JOE MATTES — Navy, World War II
STEVE MATTES — Coast Guard, Vietnam War
ANTHONY PADULA — Army, Vietnam War

Relatives who are currently serving:

CHRIS LUSSIER — Air Force
FRED PADULA — Navy
DOUG BROWN — Air Force

PREFACE

I have never served in the United States Armed Forces, but I have served as a missionary abroad. I know what it feels like to be in a foreign country when your child is going through a difficult time, and you are not there to help them. While serving as a missionary, I missed family events and have been in some dangerous situations. It was during these times that my faith was tested, and I learned to solely lean on God's promises. I developed "battle plans" and lists of songs to help me stay optimistic—praying and reading God's word was paramount because that was how He spoke to me. He never failed to encourage me, warn me, or protect me. Each trip I took changed my perspective of life and showed me the things in life that are really important. I know that my situation is nothing like what people in the military face, but what I do know is that God can help us overcome the repercussions of anything we have faced in the past, or situations we are currently facing. While praying one day for our veterans and for those who are currently serving our country, God laid it on my heart to write this book. The desire grew stronger daily and I continued to seek the Lord because I had no idea what I was supposed to write. As I spent time each day in God's word, He always gave me something to write about.

This book has a daily devotion with a battle strategy and a battle song to help you fight the attacks from the enemy of your soul. Throughout history, music was played before, after, and during battles.

For me, Christian battle songs are a big part of my success in overcoming whatever I am facing. Listening to my battle playlist when I am too overwhelmed to read or pray brings me the peace and encouragement I need to persevere. I pray that as you read the daily devotions, listen to the battle songs, and use the listed battle strategies, that God speaks to your heart and gives you the courage, strength, and guidance you need to conquer whatever is holding you back from moving forward into the next season of your life. I strongly suggest that you create your own playlist of the battle songs that apply to your situation and that you develop a battle plan to fight the enemy of despair. Remember you are warrior—fight and never give up until the enemy is defeated!!

TO EVERYTHING THERE IS A
SEASON, A TIME FOR EVERY
PURPOSE UNDER HEAVEN
—ECCLESIASTES 3:1

1

FIGHTING THE ELEMENTS OF THE SEASON

Each season has a specific purpose that contributes to the success of life on Earth. Similarly, the cycles in a person's life change. As children, we learn about life and the world around us, and we eventually grow into adulthood. As adults, we decide what we will do with our lives and how we will contribute to society. As we reach our senior years, we may retire from our professions and hopefully get to enjoy the fruits of our labor. However, this does not mean that we retire from life itself.

Within each person's life span, there are many seasons. Just as winter, spring, summer, and fall come every year bringing sunshine, rain, heat, and cold, life brings a variety of happiness, sorrow, peace, and turmoil. The sun does not always shine; depending on where you live you can also expect rain and thunderstorms, or perhaps tornados, hurricanes, or typhoons. Therefore, we tend to plan our activities according to the season and the weather. People consider the forecast before beginning their day because meteorological conditions affect visibility, alter terrain, and pose other dangerous hazards. As such, we must strategically plan our day, all while contemplating the risks.

What happens, however, when people plan everything perfectly and an unexpected storm causes devastation anyway? Some people panic, some people instantly go into survival mode, while others seek help. Likewise, as much as we plan for the future, there is still uncertainty because of the outside forces that affect our trajectory. Therefore, it is how we adapt to the unexpected that makes all the difference—it will determine how we weather the chaos; do we pridefully say, "I got this" when the house is filling up with flood waters or do we ask someone with a boat to rescue us? It is okay to ask for help; remember soldiers depend on one another to win wars, and once they achieve victory, they teach others how to defeat the enemy. So, the question is: *What season are you in today and how are you adapting to the elements?*

BATTLE PLAN: It is inevitable that during one of the seasons of our lives, we will experience unexpected storms of change, fear, and uncertainty. However, God's love for His children will never change; He promises to help us overcome anything we encounter—if we ask Him to and we don't give up. Even though I cannot see the wind, I feel it, I see its impact and I know it exists. I have never seen God, but I can feel Him, and I have seen the impact He has made in my life and in the world around me. Through surrendering, trusting, persevering, and believing, I received miracles and I obtained healing, peace, and joy through times of injury, illness, uncertainty, and despair. You can have this too, if you choose to open your heart and mind to what God has for you! The only time defeat is inevitable is when we surrender, so fight—never give up!

BATTLE SONG: "The Elements" by TobyMac

A TIME TO BE BORN, AND A
TIME TO DIE—ECCLESIASTES 3:2

WHO AM I?

"For You formed my inward parts; You covered me in my mother's womb. I will praise You, for I am fearfully and wonderfully Made" - Psalm 139:13-14a (NKJ)

When God created us, He had a specific purpose for each of our lives. As He formed our anatomy and personality, He left an empty space in our hearts that He would fill. He also instilled special gifts inside of us that made each of us unique. Therefore, He knows exactly who we are and who He wants us to become. However, sometimes **we** have no idea who we are, or what our purpose in life is.

If the world was a perfect place and the people in it were also perfect there would always be love, peace, and joy. Sometimes we do find ourselves in a season where all is well and filled with these things: our relationships are great, our finances are great, and our health is great. During times like this we are confident, happy, and productive. However, when one or more of these things is not going well, we often lose our joy and peace and start replacing them with worry and fear. This is when the enemy of our soul starts attacking our minds, firing heavy artillery at us, just like any other enemy would do when they see a weakness in their foe.

When the war begins, we do our best to stay positive and use our worldly knowledge and understanding of the situation to prepare for battle and fight against the attacks. Unfortunately, sometimes there is a domino effect where one problem causes another and then another. When anxiety and hopelessness take over, we begin to lose our identity as well. Sometimes, instead of fighting harder, we give up. All the while, God is trying to get our attention saying, *"ask me for help; I have already conquered this enemy and I can lead you to victory."* Other times He whispers, *this battle is mine, sit back and watch me perform a miracle."* Sometimes the wait is short and other times it is long because God wants to build our faith and stamina. Maybe He has put people in our life that can help us win the war because they have fought a similar battle and won. It is our choice to accept the help. Picture yourself in a physical war against a foreign enemy, would you refuse help? When we accept help from God or others and begin to win battle after battle, we become stronger and even more confident than we were before the war even started because we realize who we truly are—a child of the living God, the creator of heaven and earth, who loves us and has promised to never leave us (Deuteronomy 31:8).

BATTLE PLAN: When Satan was thrown out of heaven, he planned to fill the place in our hearts that was meant for God. If that space is empty, it is easier for Satan to occupy it. Once he is there, he often disguises himself as fear, pride, or unbelief, so we don't recognize it's him. If God is in that place, there will be a battle to win control over it. God does not expect us to fight this war on our own; "not by might or by power, but by My Spirit says the Lord" (Zechariah 4:6 NIV). Our part is to ask God for help, believe in His word, and follow His lead. Just like any superior helps those under their command, God will help us if we are His! It is never too late for us to receive the inheritance that God has set aside for us. Once we know who God is, we will truly know who we are! The poet E. Mary Grimes said this about God:

> He will silently plan for you,
> His object of omniscient care;
> God himself undertakes to be
> Your Pilot through each subtle snare.
>
> He will silently plan for you
> So certainly, He cannot fail!
> Rest on the faithfulness of God
> In Him you surely will prevail.
>
> He will silently plan for you
> Some wonderful surprise of love
> No eye has seen, nor ear has heard
> But it is kept for you above.
>
> He will silently plan for you,
> His purposes will all unfold;
> Your tangled life will shine at last,
> A masterpiece of skill untold.

He will silently plan for you,
Happy child of a Father's care,
As if no other claimed His love,
But you alone to Him were dear.

BATTLE SONG: "Who Am I" by Casting Crowns

SOMEDAY:
A DANGEROUS WORD

"What then? Shall we sit idly down and say the night has come; it is no longer day? Yet as the evening twilight fades away the sky is filled with stars, invisible to day"—
Nathaniel William Taylor

The word "someday" in the dictionary is defined as, "some unspecified time in the future." We hear people use this word in sentences like someday I will spend more time with my family; someday I will get help; someday I will start exercising and eating better. Perhaps the definition of "someday" should be, *Things we know we should do today, but don't make time for.*

There are so many things that prevent us from accomplishing what we want to do. Some of these things are out of our control due to accidents, illness, unemployment, hurricanes, etc. Even though these things can be devastating, God has allowed them to happen to fulfill a purpose that He has for us. Chester Nimitz was an admiral in the US Navy during World War II and wrote this about life:

> I asked God for strength that I might achieve. I was made weak that I might learn to obey. I asked for health that I might do great things. I was given infirmity that I might do better things. I asked for riches that I might be happy. I was given poverty that I might be wise. I asked for power that I might have the praise of men. I was given weakness that I might feel the need of God. I asked for all things that I might enjoy life. I was given life that I might enjoy all things. I got nothing I asked for, but everything I hoped for. Almost despite myself, my unspoken prayers were answered. I am, among all men, most richly blessed.

God created human beings to be smarter than any other created thing. This can be a blessing, but sometimes a curse because we believe that we know what is best for us. When our brilliant plans fail, we need to evaluate where we are in life and why we are there —

then we should ask God to guide us. He created the universe; nothing is too hard for Him. Admiral Nimitz did not get what he asked for because God had better things in mind for him and He does for us.

As human beings, we are aware that death will come for us all "someday." For some people that date could be 50 years away, yet for some it could be tomorrow. When we realize that our time has run out and we cannot fulfill our "someday wish list," what thoughts will be running through our minds—more importantly, where will we spend eternity?! These are very important questions that do not belong on a list that we will fulfill someday in the future.

BATTLE PLAN: If the enemy (Satan) can keep you unproductive, he doesn't have to worry about you. Therefore, he will send thoughts, people, or situations to delay your progress. Once he gets you to procrastinate, he finishes you off with a round of guilt for putting things off. Recognize these tactics—you are a warrior and your mission in life is not over. Don't surrender now. Just because you can't see the stars during the day, it doesn't mean they are not in the sky. God is with you too, even though you can't see Him; He may not give you what you ask for, but He will give you what you need to win this battle.

BATTLE SONG: "Move (Keep Walkin')" by TobyMac

WHEN WE WANT TO DIE

"I am prepared to meet my Maker. Whether my Maker is prepared for the great ordeal of meeting me is another matter" —Winston Churchill

Have you ever heard somebody call a woman a Jezebel? If you look the name up online, the Word Hippo website's definition of Jezebel is: "An evil scheming or shameless woman." Did you know that there really was such a woman named Jezebel? She was the wife of King Ahab, who began ruling the Northern Kingdom of Israel around 874 B.C. He was evil, but not as evil as his wife!

King Ahab and Queen Jezebel had many prophets who worshiped the false god Baal. Elijah was one of God's prophets and he ended up killing all the prophets of Baal. When Jezebel found out what Elijah had done, she sent a messenger to Elijah saying, "So let the gods do to me and more also, if I do not make your life as the life of one of them by tomorrow about this time.'" Elijah ran for his life and stopped by a tree and prayed that God would take his life, but He didn't. An angel appeared to him and gave him some food. Elijah walked for 40 days and spent the night in a cave (1 Kings 19:1-5 NKJ). It was there that he was told to "go out and stand on the mountain before the Lord" (1 Kings 19:11 NKJ), so he did.

"The Lord passed by, and a great strong wind tore into the mountains and broke the rocks in pieces before the Lord, but the Lord was not in the wind; and after the wind an earthquake, but the Lord was not in the earthquake; and after the earthquake a fire, but the Lord was not in the fire; and after the fire a still small voice" (1 Kings 19:11-12 NKJ).

We would think that God's voice would have been loud and condemning, but it wasn't—it was gentle. He knew what His prophet had been through. God did not grant Elijah's request to die. Instead, God spoke to Elijah on the mountain, and He gave him guidance and protection to complete his mission. Some may think this is just a story and might not be true, but the Old Testament is an account of Jewish History. I can relate to Elijah because I once asked God to take my life too, but He didn't.

My daughter almost died when she was in the 11th grade. It was a hard time for me: my husband and I were separated and my mom, who was my best friend, had Alzheimer's that was getting worse. Nobody knew that I was struggling because I was active in my church and the community—I hid my hopeless state well. One day I tried to take my life, but I started vomiting and passed out. I woke up to the police banging on my door. God wasn't ready to meet me in Heaven. When I look back at all I have accomplished with and through the Lord over the past 22 years, I know why He kept me alive, and I am so glad that He did. I am sharing this story because life can be so overwhelming at times, and we want to give up. However, I now realize why God chooses the day we die; it's because He knows the beginning from the end, and we don't. God's plans for us are good, not bad, and things will get better if we stay close to Him, trust Him, and don't give up!

BATTLE PLAN: The enemy of our soul is relentless; he wants to annihilate us and do whatever it takes to get us alone and defeated. We must recognize this tactic—when it starts happening, we are in the worst place we could be. When soldiers on the battlefield find themselves alone, they know they are in trouble. However, when the battle is in their mind and not physical, they tend to fight that battle alone. No matter where we are in our lives, God can transform us. When we resist the devil's lies and focus on God's promises, we can not only secure our victory, but we can help others find their way out of their season of despair as well.

BATTLE SONG: "Oh My Soul" by Casting Crowns

A New Life

"Just as Christ was raised from the dead by the glory of the Father, even so we also should walk in newness of life." —Romans 6:4 (NKJ)

A ruler/commander has the authority to allow circumstances to affect, or not affect those they rule. If those they lead do not follow orders, there are usually consequences for their actions. Sometimes God's children, who say they have surrendered their lives to Him, refuse to yield control over certain parts of their lives. Can you imagine if military personnel had this type of attitude regarding their commanding officer? There would be chaos and uncertainty because orders would not be followed, due to their lack of trust in their superior. Similarly, when we ignore God's commandments, our lives become full of confusion and indecisiveness, mostly because we use our emotions as a compass instead of God's word.

King David of Israel decided to stay home from the battlefield one day and ended up committing adultery and then murder. Yet, he was still known as "a man after God's own heart" (1 Samuel 13:14) because he repented and turned back to God. Since David lived before Jesus was born, he had to fulfill all the Jewish laws in order to go to Heaven when he died. Nowadays, people who accept Jesus Christ as their Lord and Savior no longer live under the law because Jesus paid for their sins on the cross and they are covered by His blood. When they sin, they need to ask God for forgiveness and repent their actions. Once they are on the right path, God can guide them and use their mistakes of the past to teach them and others about His grace and mercy.

Just like the head of a military command post has the technology to monitor the enemy's position, God is able to see what is ahead of us. He knows where the devil is and where the landmines are. He also knows our strengths, weaknesses, and what we can achieve. No matter what life situation we are currently experiencing, God can equip us with what we need to persevere. What our enemy meant for harm, He can turn into good. Our part is to seek His will and be obedient to His orders. When we do, we can *"walk in newness of life"* and not only find healing, but also make a difference in the world.

BATTLE PLAN: If I were your enemy, I would do everything to prevent you from having *"newness of life."* I would launch missiles of self-pity, hopelessness, and resentment at you. On top of that, I would convince you that your problems were God's fault, and He was your enemy. Then I would block access for you to have a relationship with any of His people because it is the one sheep that is off on its own that the wolf can conquer. It is so important for us to know who our enemy truly is: Satan. We must do everything in our power to recognize where the attacks on us are coming from. We need to ask God to help us win the battle and send reinforcements when we need them. Once we accept the situation we are in and ask God for help, He can strengthen us and provide what we need to break free from Satan's bondage.

BATTLE SONG: "Walking Free" by Micah Tyler

SACRIFICE & GUILT

"There is no greater love than to lay down one's life for one's friends"—*John 15:13 NLT*

There are many dangerous professions: working on a police force, for a fire department, or serving in the military are a few examples of these jobs. Each time one of these employees begin their day, they know it could be their last day alive. Yet, they still venture out to help and protect others. If one of these brave men or women were to lose their life, it would be a tremendous loss to society, and their death should never be in vain. The mission must still go on!

In 2013, I met a woman from Uganda named Edith at a Bible study; she was in America because her deaf daughter was getting cochlear implants that would allow her to hear. It was Edith and her husband's desire to go back home and start a nonprofit organization that would allow other deaf children to get the surgery. They found a teacher named Carrie who had a degree in deaf education, that was willing to go to Uganda. However, they needed somebody with medical knowledge to meet with the surgeons to determine what was needed to make their dream a reality. I prayed, sought God, and got confirmation to be a part of their vision. This would be the first time I was traveling to a third-world country without a mission team. I would be flying from Boston to Uganda on July 3, 2014 by myself and landing at the Entebbe Airport at 10:50 pm. Edith's flight left Boston on July 2nd; Carrie was flying out of NY on July 3rd and landing in Uganda at 2:00 pm. Edith's husband was staying in America with his daughter.

I received opposition from family and friends because the situation in Africa was very volatile at the time: Ebola was spreading, ISIS named a caliphate, and Boko Haram had kidnapped 276 girls. Edith, Carrie, and I would be spending the summer in a house we rented on the outskirts of Kampala in a Muslim neighborhood. The morning I left for Uganda, my brother called and told me to turn on my television. The US Embassy warned that there was a confirmed terrorist threat on the Entebbe Airport between 9:00 and 11:00 that night. I prayed and felt that God still wanted me to go, so I did. We

16

spent the summer traveling throughout Uganda visiting schools for the deaf and hospitals. God protected us, and our mission was a success. A few years later, two Ugandan children received cochlear implants and more have had the surgery since then. Sometimes, however, things don't go as planned and there are casualties. When this happens, we often focus on the *I should have done that scenario*. It's healthy to evaluate what happened and learn from it, but then we must move on. Guilt/regret does not come from God; Jesus died for us sacrificially, so we could have eternal life, but also *abundant life* on earth, not a life of regrets (John 10:10). Are you living life to the fullest? If not, you need to let God help you let go of the past.

BATTLE PLAN: When I was in Uganda, I was ridden with guilt when I missed my daughter's birthday and when I wasn't there for her when her boyfriend broke up with her. I had to seek God daily for reassurance and encouragement that I was doing the right thing, Then I had to trust God to take care of my daughter, while I was on the mission field fighting for those who were being oppressed. I went to Uganda knowing the dangers. If I died on the trip, I would have wanted the mission to continue. If Edith felt that my death was her fault because she asked me to go and her guilt prevented her from continuing, my death would have been meaningless. People who serve in the armed forces are often victims of survivor's guilt. They may also feel remorse if they were injured and had to leave their buddies on the battlefield. Guilt can be crippling, and Satan loves to use this weapon to prevent people from forgiving themselves and being effective in the world. We must remember that we are still alive because God has a plan for our lives. George S. Patton said, "It is foolish and wrong to mourn the men who died. Rather we should thank God that such men lived." So, let's thank God for them and honor them by giving everything we have to God's vision for our lives— while leaving any guilt we feel at the foot of the cross!

BATTLE SONG: "What if I Gave Everything" by Casting Crowns

WALKING THROUGH DEATH'S VALLEY

"Yea, though I walk through the valley of the shadow of death, I will fear no evil; for You are with me; Your rod and Your staff, they comfort me." —Psalm 23:4

Even people who have never read the Bible have most likely heard the above scripture before. Those who have dangerous jobs especially find comfort in the Psalmist's words. I personally experienced the shadow of death when I was diagnosed with cancer. When I was on the mission field, I experienced the shadow of death, fear, and evil at the same time. Knowing that God was with me during those times gave me comfort and the strength to keep going.

Ironically, as Christians, sometimes death seems better than what we are currently experiencing because we know that we will be in Heaven when we die and there will be no more pain or sorrow. Nevertheless, God still has us here for a reason and we need to seek God continually to see how He wants us to proceed. Sometimes He shows us something we may have done to cause our dilemma and what we need to do to fix the problem. However, other times we have no idea why we are in our situation. All we feel is the Lord's painful nudges from His staff prompting us to move in the right direction, just like a shepherd does to his sheep. What we must remember is that the shepherd's love and desire to defend the flock is his number one priority. Similarly, God's staff guides us, and His rod protects us from dangerous predators who want to destroy us, so we never have to fear the valley because we are not alone.

BATTLE PLAN: Jesus said, "I am the good Shepherd. The good Shepherd gives His life for the sheep. But a hireling, he who is not the Shepherd, one who does not own the sheep, sees the wolf coming and leaves the sheep and flees; and the wolf catches the sheep and scatters them" (John 10:11-12 NKJ). There are so many false "securities" in the world: drugs and alcohol are a couple of the "hirelings." They are a temporary escape from reality, but often cause pain and death rather than protection and comfort. Many of us heard the Little Red Riding Hood fairy tale when we were children. The wolf in the story disguised himself as the girl's grandmother. There is a powerful lesson in that fable: things are not always what they appear to be. On the contrary, God will always be who He claims to be—our Heavenly Father who loves us and wants the best for us! This knowledge is all we need to bring us comfort when we must walk through the valley.

BATTLE SONG: "I just need U" by TobyMac

DYING TO SELF

"I count him braver who overcomes his desire than him who conquers his enemies; for the hardest victory is over self."—Aristotle

We all have an agenda and hopefully goals for the future; we often plan our life around them. While it is important to have dreams, we can't be deceived into thinking: *if I owned my own business, I would be happy; if I could find the perfect spouse, I would be happy; if I was healthy, I would be happy;* and the list goes on and on. Unfortunately, God's goals and deadlines often conflict with ours.

I once heard someone say that happiness is fleeting. Although this is true, it does not mean that we shouldn't enjoy those fleeting moments in life. In addition, we should come to the realization that no matter how many material things we acquire, how many great relationships we form, or how good our health is, we will probably find something else to complain about. This is because when God created us, He put a place in our hearts that only He could fill. If we try to put other things in that spot, we will still feel the emptiness. However, once we allow God to take His proper place in our lives, He completes us because He can fill us with hope when we are in despair, peace when life is uncertain, and strength when we are weak.

The ways of this world are so different than the ways of Christianity. With Christianity, we are called to "count it all joy when we fall into various trials" (James 1:2 NKJ). Whereas the world teaches us to be happy only when everything in life is good. God uses the storms to build up our endurance and our faith. Someone training for a marathon doesn't run only when the weather is good; they run in all types of weather to condition themselves for what they may encounter during the race. God knows the path ahead of us and He knows exactly the type of training we need. Theologian and poet Thomas Traherne once said, "Till you are familiar with the ways of God in all ages as with your walk and table…you never enjoy the world." So, how do we get to this place? We arrive there when we let go of our fleshly desires that are hindering us from finding true joy in the Lord.

BATTLE PLAN: Aristotle was a Greek scientist and philosopher who was known to be the most brilliant "thinker" of his time. He totally understood that self-will was the hardest thing for us to conquer, especially when it comes to addictions that are not good for us. Thomas Traherne also said, "Till you can sing and rejoice and delight in God, as misers do in gold, and kings in scepters, you never enjoy the world." It is dying to our will and asking God to show us His purpose for our life that will bring joy. When we use our warrior skills to overcome our desires and make it a priority to seek God's word and His will for us instead, we will have peace no matter what life brings our way. God loves us, and He will always equip us with what we need to fulfill our purpose.

BATTLE SONG: "Letting Go" by Jeremy Camp

THE PART OF US THAT LIVES ON

"The only thing that walks back from the tomb with the mourners and refuses to be buried is the character of a man. What a man is survives him. It can never be buried."—J. R. Miller

This week I watched a congressional hearing about corruption in the United States government. Many of us see changes going on in the world that are shocking. It appears that there is a fight to take away some of the Constitutional freedoms that Americans are entitled to. Some people are speaking out against this attempt, and they are being persecuted for their actions. The persecution of people and the determination of those persecuted to do the right thing has been happening for thousands of years. Hopefully, people will learn from history.

In the Old Testament of the Bible, David was anointed by the prophet Samuel to be king (2 Samuel 2:4), because King Saul disobeyed God's orders. The spirit of God left Saul and the empty spot inside of him that was once filled with God was taken over by an evil spirit that tormented him (1 Samuel 16:14). David was very loyal to Saul; however, Saul became jealous of David's popularity and set out to destroy him. One day David was hiding in a cave from Saul and he cried out to the Lord for help saying, "Be merciful to me, O God, be merciful to me! For my soul trusts in You, and in the shadow of Your wings I will make my refuge, until these calamities have passed by. I will cry out to God Most High, to God who performs all things for me. He shall send from heaven and save me; He reproaches the one who would swallow me up. God shall send forth His mercy and His truth. I lie among the sons of men who are set on fire, whose teeth are spears and arrows. And their tongue a sharp sword…They have prepared a net for my steps; my soul is bowed down; they have dug a pit before me; *into the midst of it they themselves have fallen*" (Psalm 57:1-4,6 NKJ). God came to David's rescue. God will be with us too when we are doing the honorable thing. It does not mean that God will always deliver us from our enemies; sometimes He strengthens us to persevere until the appointed time.

Author C. S. Lewis said, "You never know how much you really believe anything until its truth or falsehood becomes a matter of life and death to you." When God made David king He said, "I have found David son of Jesse, a man after my own heart; he will do what I want him to do" (Acts 13:22 NLT). However, David committed adultery and murder, but he repented and lived the rest of his life honoring God. It was David's lineage that Jesus Christ came from. David's honorable character is still mentioned today. King Saul disobeyed God and later found himself in a battle with the Philistines; he was afraid of being captured, so he took his own life (1 Samule 31:4). Saul never repented for his disobedience to God. His cowardly character is still spoken of today, and his lineage was wiped out. Who do we mostly resemble: David or Saul?

BATTLE PLAN: Satan has free reign in this world (2 Corinthians 4:4), and he has many people afraid to speak the truth; he has others focused on power. God is not surprised when we fail (Romans 8:23). However, if we do, we need to repent like David did and honor God. The Bible tells us to "have nothing to do with the fruitless deeds of darkness, but rather expose them" (Ephesians 5:11 NIV). It is important that we pray and seek God's guidance on how He wants us to proceed. Sometimes, God has us hiding from evil, sometimes He has us praying/waiting, and other times He has us moving and exposing. Either way, we can be sure of God's promise to be with us always. When we pray and seek God, the best part of us will live on when we die.

BATTLE SONG: "Legacy" by Nicole Nordeman

THE DEATH OF THE ENEMY

"Only the dead have seen the end of war."—Plato

There are many books published about the battlefield of the mind. Perhaps the struggles within us are harder to conquer than any physical attacks against us. When someone physically attacks us, our instincts take over and we immediately try to protect ourselves. This can consist of running away from the attacker or fighting back with all our might. However, when our mind is being attacked with memories of the past or fear of the future, we often find it difficult to escape the assault. At times like this, we need to focus on God's promises and seek His help.

The apostle Paul and Silas were beaten and thrown into jail in Philippi. They chose to take any thoughts of fear captive. "At midnight Paul and Silas were praying and singing hymns to God, and the prisoners were listening to them. Suddenly, there was a great earthquake, so that the foundations of the prison were shaken, and immediately all the doors were opened, and everyone's chains were loosed. And the keeper of the prison, awakening from sleep and seeing the prison doors open, supposing the prisoners had fled, drew his sword and was about to kill himself. But Paul called out with a loud voice, saying 'Do yourself no harm, for we are all here.' Then he called for a light, ran in, and fell down trembling before Paul and Silas and he brought them out and said, 'Sirs, what must I do to be saved?' So they said, 'Believe in the Lord Jesus Christ, and you will be saved, you and your household'" (Acts 16:25-30 NKJ). Paul and Silas were released from prison the next day and the enemy, Satan, was defeated.

Paul and Silas were singing because their trust was in God. They focused on their mission not their circumstances, and God came to their rescue. Paul told the people of Corinth, "For the weapons we fight with are not the weapons of the world. On the contrary, they have divine power to demolish strongholds" (2 Corinthians 10:4 NIV). Paul knew that his war, although at times was physical, was against spiritual forces. This is also true of wars that the military physically fights when they are trying to free people from communist countries; it is the evil forces of Satan that are controlling the dictator. As Plato's quote states, we will be in a spiritual battle until the day we die.

The enemy of our soul wants us to join forces with him, and if we don't, he will do everything thing in his power to annihilate us or to take us out of the fight. His methods of torture are not physical, they are mental. God can help us fight the enemy, just like he helped Paul and Silas. Our part is to seek His guidance, pray, and sing.

BATTLE PLAN: During the Vietnam War there was a propaganda radio broadcast by a North Vietnamese woman the US Troops called, Hanoi Hannah. The goal of this program was to mess with the minds of the American military who were fighting for the South Vietnamese. Hannah would list names of Americans that died fighting and talk about the protests of the war going on in America. She knew that breaking someone's spirit and their will to fight could be very effective during a war. It is one of Satan's oldest tactics and he still uses it today to defeat us. Through depression and anxiety attacks, the enemy breaks our morale; it is during these times that we must focus on the truth— God is for us and with us and He will help us. We must recognize the propaganda the devil is filling our minds with and replace those thoughts with God's words of truth. We are warriors and God has good plans for our future and not evil (Jeremiah 29:11).

BATTLE SONG: "Surrounded (Fight My Battles)" by Michael W. Smith

A TIME TO PLANT, AND A TIME
TO PLUCK WHAT IS PLANTED
—ECCLESIASTES 3:2B

PLANT SEEDS OF TRUST

"Farmers who wait for the perfect weather never plant. If they watch every cloud, they never harvest. Just as you cannot understand the path of the wind or the mystery of a tiny baby growing in its mother's womb, so you cannot understand the activity of God, who does all things. Plant your seed in the morning and keep busy all afternoon, for you don't know if profit will come from one activity or another—or maybe both"—Ecclesiastes 11:4-6 (NLT)

Soldiers are always taking risks while they are on a mission. They cannot always wait for the perfect weather or circumstances because time may be of the essence. This scenario is also true in civilian life. We often have a desire or hunch to do something, however, once we start contemplating the stakes, we often miss golden opportunities.

My dad grew up during the great depression. When he finished school, he enlisted in the Navy and fought in World War II. When the war ended and he came home, he was offered the opportunity to invest in the very first Dunkin' Donuts, which was in Quincy, Massachusetts. As he was considering this venture, he started thinking logically: *"who in their right mind would leave their house to pay for a cup of coffee, when they can make it at home for free?"* Human reasoning was not the only thing that kept him from investing—the darkness of fear was also penetrating his perception. Some say that our past experiences make us who we are today. As such, my father was very careful about how he spent his money, but also very generous to others.

Fear is an emotion that can prevent us from moving forward in any area of our life: it clouds our discernment and leaves God out of the equation. My father chose to play it safe and not invest in Dunkin' Donuts, but every time he drove by one, he had regrets. That is exactly how the enemy of your soul works: he instills fear and then beats you up for being afraid to do something. God on the other hand, will give you clarity of mind and instill peace when He wants us to move in a certain direction, but...only if we ask Him to give us wisdom and guidance. "If any of you lacks wisdom, let him ask of God, who gives to all liberally and without reproach, and it will be given to him. But let him ask in faith, with no doubting, for he who doubts is like a wave of the sea driven and tossed by the wind. For let not that man suppose that he will receive anything from the Lord; he is a double-minded man, unstable in all his ways" (James 1:5-8 NKJ). Living by this scripture has been a huge blessing in my life! When I pray about something, I ask God to align my desires with His. I also ask Him to shut all the doors that He does not want me to enter and open the door that He wants me to go through. When I do this, it takes doubt totally out of the equation because I am giving God permission to intervene. How do you make your decisions?

BATTLE PLAN: As human beings, we always want to be in control of our own life. However, we must remember that we are constantly in a spiritual battle between good and evil. This means that sometimes God wants to give us great opportunities and Satan instills fear that causes us to walk away from a blessing. People in the armed forces are taught to follow orders and trust their commander because they have vital information that their men/woman are not privy to. Likewise, God knows what is ahead of us and "withholds not good thing from those who walk uprightly" (Psalm 84:11 NKJ). Therefore, let's plant seeds of trust in our heavenly commander-in-chief and not let fear prevent us from living life to the fullest.

BATTLE SONG: "No Longer Slaves" by Zach Williams

PLANT SEEDS OF TRUTH

"Whatever things are true, whatever things are noble, whatever things are just, whatever things are pure, whatever things are lovely, whatever things are of good report, if there is any virtue and if there is anything praiseworthy—meditate on these things. The things which you learned and received and heard and saw in me, these do, and the God of peace will be with you" —Philippians 4:8-9 NKJ

Farmers do not throw seeds up in the air and let them land where they may; instead, they strategically plan where to place them. When considering what to plant they take many things into consideration like climate, soil, sun, and rain. They immediately reject the idea of planting things that are not good for the conditions needed to grow bountiful crops. Tilling the soil, sowing the seeds, and harvesting the crops is a lot of work. This same theory can also be applied to other professions, as well as our spiritual growth.

The human brain controls many things: emotions, thoughts, memories, and other processes that regulate our body. We have no control over some of these functions. However, with God's help we can learn to discipline our thoughts. This may not always be an easy thing to do, especially when it is a memory of something we have experienced. When a thought enters our mind, we can choose to think about it or choose to focus on something else. Our strategy to take control over what we contemplate is much like that of a farmer—it takes planning and work. Philippians 4:8-9 above gives us instructions on how to do this.

When I was diagnosed with ovarian cancer, I had a choice on how I would process the information. Did the news mean I was going to die? No, not necessarily! Plenty of people survive cancer. Did it mean that I was going to go through pain? No, some people do not get sick from chemo and radiation. In fact, I knew people who were actually healed by God. Some did not have to go through treatment, and some did. One person I know was told by the medical professionals that they did all they could for him and there was nothing else they could do. However, someone prayed over him, and he was totally healed. As such, I took my thoughts captive when I heard my diagnosis and focused on what was "of good report." The truth was that my cancer could have fallen into any one of the above scenarios, so I decided to believe that God would heal me—and He did! I did not even have to go through treatment.

The opening scripture states that we have a part to play in obtaining God's peace: we must take our thoughts captive, believe His promises, meditate on them, and then yield control of our situation to Him.

BATTLE PLAN: When we find ourselves thinking of worse-case scenarios, we should do what the farmer does—immediately reject the things that will not grow to produce a good sound mind: fear, worry, and despair. Then we must plant seeds of truth, hope, and faith in their place and ask God to water them and watch them grow. They will yield bushels of peace!

BATTLE SONG: "Overcomer" by Mandisa

PLANTS SEEDS OF HOPE

"Let us not become weary in doing good, for at the proper time we will reap a harvest if we do not give up"—Galatians 6:9 (NIV)

We often experience a season of discouragement because we let people's opinions cause us to doubt our purpose. It is during times like this that we must not give up. Did you know that Albert Einstein almost dropped out of college because his grades were so bad? Upon graduating college, he could only get a job as a traveling insurance agent. However, his resilience and desire to persevere paid off and he was eventually awarded the Nobel Prize in Physics. People sometimes use the phrase *"they are not an Einstein"* when they are referring to someone that is not very smart. Einstein, who was known to be a student with no potential in college, is now considered by some to be the most brilliant man ever born. If I had a question on the theory of relativity, I would have asked Einstein, because he developed it and created the laws of physics. Since God created us and the world around us, wouldn't it be wise for us to ask Him if we need knowledge and guidance in our life?

Jeremiah 29:11-13 (NKJ) says, "For I know the thoughts that I think toward you, says the Lord, thoughts of peace and not of evil, to give you a future and a hope. Then you will call upon Me and go and pray to Me, and I will listen to you. And you will seek Me and find Me, when you search for Me with all your heart." This promise tells us that God has plans for our lives and He is waiting for us to ask Him about them. What season of your life are you in? Are you plucking the rewards of hard work that you planted, or are you still unsure about what type of seeds to plant? Either way, why not sow seeds of hope and faith in God because, like the farmer, we always harvest what we plant.

BATTLE PLAN: Einstein may have failed some subjects in college, but he was brilliant when it came to science. We should not let people define who we are because we do not fit into their "description" of what is intelligent. The Bible says that "God chose the foolish things of the world to shame the wise; God chose the weak things of the world to shame the strong (1 Corinthians 1:27 NIV). I think the professors who thought Einstein would fail, probably felt pretty dumb when he received the Nobel Prize. Theologian Margaret Bottome said, "Christ's triumph was in humiliation. And perhaps our triumph will also be revealed through what others see as humiliation." Satan knows the Bible states "Where there is no vision, the people perish" (Proverbs 29:18 KJV). Therefore, he wants to convince us that the vision we have is not from God. As such, he will often place people in our paths to discourage us from moving forward. Nevertheless, when God gives us a vision, He will equip us with night-vision goggles, so that we can see the deeds of darkness coming up against us. We must remember Romans 8:24 (NIV): "Hope that is seen is no hope at all. Who hopes for what they already have?" Remember, just because we can't see anything materializing, doesn't mean that it won't happen. BELIEVE!

BATTLE SONG: "I Still Believe" by Jeremy Camp

PLANTING TREES OF LOVE

"He that plants trees love others beside himself"—Thomas Fuller

Trees are extremely important for human beings' survival; they convert carbon dioxide and water into oxygen and also filter water by taking the toxins that are in the soil out. Since oxygen and water are necessary for us to survive, who knows how long people could live without trees. Aside from those two examples, trees produce food, provide shade, and house animals. In fact, they house humans as well because it is the wood from trees that we use to build houses, make furniture, and also burn in our fireplaces for heat. Studies have shown that trees actually help people stay mentally fit as well. When people take walks in the park, they not only enjoy the beauty of nature, but they are also getting exercise. For these reasons and more, God created trees.

God loved Adam and Eve and He gave them everything they needed to live a healthy and happy life. When Satan convinced Eve to eat from the Tree of Good and Evil, God banished them from the Garden of Eden. He was concerned that they would eat from the Tree of Life and live forever in disobedience (Genesis 3:22-24). Whereas God's plan for people was for them to live in Heaven for all eternity with Him and His son Jesus. A man named Job, who is written about in the Old Testament of the Bible, lost everything he owned and all of his family. In a prayer to God, he said, "At least there is hope for a tree: if it is cut down, it will sprout again, and its new shoots will not fail. Its roots may grow old in the ground and its stump die in the soil, yet at the scent of water it will bud and put forth shoots like a plant. But a man dies and is laid low; he breathes his last and is no more" (Job 14:7-10 NIV). Some trees during the days of Job did grow back when cut down and some trees today do as well; Elm, Willow, and Cottonwood trees are a few examples. Job felt there was no hope for him because he lived before the days of Jesus.

The book of Revelation states in verse 22:14 (KJV): "Blessed are they that do his commandments, that they may have the right to the tree of life and may enter in through the gates into the city." It was a tree that was used to make the cross that Jesus carried and died on, to fulfill God's plan for us to spend eternity with them. God planted all kinds of trees for us, especially the one that His Son died on because He loves us so much!

BATTLE PLAN: What is causing us to feel so hopeless today? Perhaps we are struggling to feed our families or pay our bills. There is one important fact about trees that we would be wise to embrace: trees do not grow beyond their ability to support themselves. The devil will try his best to convince us that we have to give our kids everything that they want; we need to hide the fact that we are struggling financially, so we charge expensive business meals; or that we must buy designer clothes that we can't afford because our friends wear them. When trees are stressed, they shed flowers, leaves, fruits, or branches. The theme of Psalm 1 in the Bible is about two roads of life. One road is the path that a person with faith travels and the other road is traveled by a person with no faith. Verses 1-3 in Psalm 1 (NKJ) state: "Blessed is the man who walks not in the counsel of the ungodly, nor stands in the path of sinners, nor sits in the seat of the scornful (v.1); but his delight is in the law of the LORD, and in His law he meditates day and night (v.2), He shall be like a tree planted by the rivers of water, that brings forth its fruit in its season; whose leaf also shall not wither; and whatever he does shall prosper (v3)." So, let's ask God to help us start walking on the right path!

BATTLE SONG: "Trees We'll Never See" by Amy Grant

PLANTING SUNFLOWERS & PLUCKING BLESSINGS

"Many flowers open to the sun, but only one follows him constantly. Heart, be thou the sunflower, not only open to receive God's blessing, but constant in looking to Him." —Jean Paul

The seeds from flowers grow roots that go down into the ground to secure an anchor for the plant. It is the root that stores the food and water. Once the plant is grounded a stem grows upward toward the sky, which carries the nutrients to the plant. Eventually the plant matures and produces flowers. Sunflowers have roots that go many feet into the soil, the stems that shoot up are thick to hold the big yellow flowers.

Artist Vincent van Gogh was fascinated by sunflowers and his paintings reflected their beauty and strength; he believed that these flowers brought light to the countryside. Although he suffered from depression and low self-esteem, painting sunflowers brought him joy. He once said, "What would life be if we had no courage to attempt anything." Because he was willing to ignore his insecurities and paint what was in his heart, he not only became famous, but his paintings brought a new type of painting to the industry. I guess you could say that he was *"open to receive God's blessing,"* which in return blessed many people who bought his paintings.

Helen Keller once said, "Keep your face to the sunshine and you cannot see the shadow. It's what sunflowers do." These flowers are often referred to as sun worshipers because they turn to face the sun. Similarly, when we look to the Son of God, He is able block out the dark clouds of despair and give us a ray of hope. Once we get rooted in God's word, the scriptures become the nutrients we need to grow stronger so that we can push up through the dark soil of depression into the bright sunlight.

BATTLE PLAN: Vincent van Gogh didn't let his lack of self-confidence keep him from doing what he enjoyed. The enemy wants to steal any opportunity for us to have happiness and peace. However,

God will plant desires in our hearts that will not only lead to joy but will also bring blessings to others. Van Gogh once said, "If you hear a voice within you saying, 'You are not a painter,' then by all means paint...and that voice will be silenced." We can tell the difference between the enemy's voice and God's voice because the enemy will discourage us; if that doesn't work, he will try to instill fear in us to prevent us from escaping his captivity. However, Psalm 37:4-5 states, "Delight yourself in the Lord and He will give you desires of your heart. Commit your way to the Lord, trust also in him, and he shall bring it to pass" (NKJ). Therefore, let's turn our face to the Son, like the sunflowers do and leave the dark clouds of depression behind us!

BATTLE SONG: "Sunflower" by Pauline Zoe Park

PLUCKING OUT NEGATIVE THOUGHTS

"For God has not given us a spirit of fear, but of power and of love and of a sound mind"—2 Timothy 1:7 NKJ

Planting seeds is only part of the process that is necessary to reap a good harvest; famers must also feed what they have planted to keep the vegetation alive and flourishing. Whatever you feed will grow, whatever you don't feed will perish. This theory also applies to what we feed our minds.

The above scripture says that God has given His children a "sound mind." If you google the definition of the word *sound*, you may find "sturdy and stable in nature," or "based on reason or good judgement," or "strengthened or made secure against attack." Why then, do we often feel that there is a battle raging on in our minds? We sometimes think that way because there is a fight for power going on that we may not even be aware of. Think of how easy it would be to conquer your enemy, if they did know that you existed, or if they heard you existed, but they thought you were a fallacy. It is safe to say that you would have a major advantage in the battle.

Satan's biggest weapon is people's unbelief in his existence. Therefore, when we have thoughts of anger, depression, or fear we try to figure out why we feel that way. Sometimes we blame people, our government, or even our family members for our despair—when it is the enemy of our soul trying to keep us in bondage and separate us from anybody who can help us. Be encouraged because God has equipped us with everything we need to triumph.

BATTLE STRATEGY: A loving father would never give one of his children a powerful tool to use and not include instructions on how to operate it. In fact, even when adults purchase anything at a store that runs on power, there is an instruction manual that explains all its uses and how to effectively operate the item. Do you realize that God left us a manual to navigate life as well? It's called the Bible. In this book there are instructions, warnings, encouragement, and battle strategies.

In fact, while Jesus was on earth, He often used farming parables to teach His followers. If we know that whatever we feed will grow, we need to feed our mind with positive things such as God's love for us and His promise that He will never leave us or forsake us.

BATTLE SONG: "Whom Shall I Fear" by Chris Tomlin

PLUCKING OUT THE LIES &
PLANTING THE TRUTH

"We demolish arguments and every pretension that sets itself up against the knowledge of God, and we take captive every thought to make it obedient to Christ" —2 Corinthians 10:5 (NIV)

These days our minds are constantly flooded with information, some of it true and some of it false. With the fast pace of life and its high demands, who has time to research everything? Some of us who have the time would rather spend it doing something else. Imagine how effective an enemy on the battlefield would be if they could feed their opposition information that was not only false but would eventually lead to their demise. Satan, the enemy of our soul, schemes to do that very thing. If he confuses and convinces us to think the wrong way, our decisions and actions can be driven by fear, depression, or hopelessness.

The Apostle Paul knew the devil's strategies, so he warned the people in Corinth to guard what enters their minds and controls their thoughts. Jesus said that Satan is the father of lies (John 8:44). It doesn't matter what our struggles are—addiction, unbelief, complacency, or anxiety the enemy attacks our minds to keep us in bondage, while blocking all avenues that allow us to escape our captivity. He can divide family and friends by causing us or them to get offended by something we say or do. He will fill our heads with thoughts that nobody cares about us, or we have no special gifts or good qualities. He will whisper, this is God's fault; if He really loved you, He would not allow you to be in this place. But in reality, it is not God's fault, we are the ones who ignore God's warning to stay away from drugs, alcohol, and His command to forgive others and not take offense. God never walks away from people; people walk away from God. He is always there waiting for them to turn back to Him.

BATTLE PLAN: As in any battle the morale of the soldier is paramount; therefore, when the bullets of doubt, fear, and discouragement come flying at our minds we need to deflect them and counter them with the word of God. When we remember that "we do not wrestle against flesh and blood, but against principalities, against powers, against the rulers of the darkness of this age, against spiritual hosts of wickedness in the heavenly places" (Eph 6:12 NKJ), we can put on our armor, grab our sword (which is the word of God) and our shield of faith. Remember, "He who is in you is greater than he who is in the world" (1 John 4:4). Since we have the Holy Spirit inside of us, we can demolish any hold the enemy has on us. When we put our trust in God, we can have peace of mind knowing that He will fight for us if the forces against us become too strong.

BATTLE SONG: "You Say" by Lauren Daigle

PLUCKING OUT THE TARES

"What is a weed? A plant whose virtues have never been discovered"—Ralph Waldo Emerson

Some synonyms for the word "virtue" regarding behavior are character, beliefs, or morals. When we use the word "virtue" to refer to the strength of our mind, the synonyms are braveries, courageousness, or heroisms. If you have ever planted a garden, you know that weeds (tares) are very resilient; they can steal water and nutrients from plants, and they are able to adapt to the environment. If we don't control them, they will take over all the space around and in between what we have planted. If we pull up a weed, we can also pull up a plant with it.

Jesus often talked in parables to the people. One day He said, "The kingdom of heaven is like a man who sowed good seed in his field; but while men slept, his enemy came and sowed tares among the wheat and went his way. But when the grain had sprouted and produced a crop then the tares also appeared" (Matthew 13: 24-26. NKJ). The enemy of our soul works the same way when it comes to us reading God's word, especially if we read it quickly and then move on with our day. Jesus said, "The farmer sows the word. Some people are like seed along the path, where the word is sown. As soon as they hear it, Satan comes and takes away the word that was sown in them. Others, like seed sown on the rocky places, hear the word and at once receive it with joy, but since they have no root, they last only a short time. When trouble or persecution comes because of the world, they quickly fall away. Still others, like seed sown among thorns, hear the word; but the worries of this life, the deceitfulness of wealth and the desire for the other things come in and choke the word, making it unfruitful. Others like seed sown on good soil, hear the word, accept it, and produce a crop" (Mark 4:14-20 NIV). I suppose that all of the above scenarios could take place during the different seasons of our lives. So, let's start by evaluating ourselves. —Are we a weed or a plant, and do we know our virtues? Once we know who we really are and what we truly believe we can begin the healing process. With God's help we can begin sowing seeds of faith and trust on good soil, that will reap a bountiful harvest of healing.

BATTLE PLAN: American Essayist Ralph Waldo Emerson said that weeds appear because virtue was never discovered. Ironically, it is often during our trials that we learn what we really believe. It is so easy to trust God when our life is moving along just the way we want it to. During this season we need to be on guard because this is when the devil will tempt us to accumulate more things, leaving us never satisfied. Suddenly, we find ourselves on the rocky path, because we were never really rooted in God's word and His ways. Maybe we quoted scripture to people and went to church every week, but did we believe what we said? It's like purchasing a Jeep Wrangler because we are told that it can adapt to any terrain. However, when we go off the road and find ourselves in deep mud and get stuck, we don't know what to do. Had we researched and read all the information about our jeep, we would have realized that we needed mud terrain tires, rather than all-terrain tires if we were going to be trekking through the wet muddy areas. Similarly, we need to be rooted in God's word before we find ourselves on the treacherous path because Satan can come in and "chock" the little faith we have right out of us. The time for us to be firmly planted and rooted in God's word is now, so when the tares of fear, anger, or depression overwhelm us, our virtues (beliefs) will be solid, and we will have the strength to overcome the enemy's attacks.

BATTLE SONG: "Word of Life" by Jeremy Camp

PLUCKING OUT A BROKEN TOOTH

"Putting confidence in an unreliable person in times of trouble is like chewing with a broken tooth." —Proverbs 25:19 (NLT)

I recently watched a movie called The Tooth Fairy, which was released in 2010 and starred Dwayne Johnson. In the film, Johnson played the role of a minor league hockey player, named Derek, who had the reputation of knocking out his opponent's teeth; thereby earning him the name—The Tooth Fairy. However, through a series of discouraging comments and events caused by Derek, he was sentenced to two weeks of service as a tooth fairy. Since Derek had no control over the development of his fairy wings and where he was sent, he ended up fulfilling his duties, changing his life for the better.

This movie generated memories from my childhood about losing my teeth. The first time I had a loose tooth I was scared and didn't want my dad to twist it and pull it out. However, when I woke up the next morning with a dollar under my pillow instead of the tooth I put there, I looked forward to the next time I lost a tooth—a little bit of pain and looking funny for a while was worth it. My dad took a scary situation in life for me and actually turned it into something I looked forward to happening again.

Our Heavenly Father wants to do the same thing for us when we lose our job, a relationship, or something else we are too attached to. Although the loss may cause us some fear and pain, we need to trust Him. Once God replaces our loss with something or someone better, we may even look forward to the next time we lose something because we know God has something better for us.

BATTLE PLAN: The enemy of our soul wants to put our trust in unreliable sources so that he can always keep us disappointed. However, we know that God wants what is best for us because Jesus said the following to the people: "If you sinful people know how to give good gifts to your children, how much more will your heavenly Father give good gifts to those who ask him" (Matthew 7:11 NLT).

Sometimes letting go of something that is part of us is painful and scary, but when we trust and believe that God has something better for us, we are able to let go easier and even look forward to what He will bring us.

BATTLE SONG: "Let Go" by Matt Hammitt

A TIME TO KILL, AND A TIME TO HEAL
—ECCLESIASTES 3:3A

KILLING THE DESIRE FOR PERFECTION

"This is the very perfection of a man, to find out his own imperfections." — *Saint Augustine*

People in the world today put high expectations on others regarding perfection. We must always say the right thing, act the right way, and believe that certain things are the truth. However, who is determining the definition of what is good or true? There are different political parties, different sexes, and different religions that all have different viewpoints. Some people seem to be perfect, according to world standards, until we find out later that they committed a crime, lied under oath, or plagiarized someone's work. Sometimes people's goals are not to be deceitful, but rather to just fit in with society and they do bad things in desperation. Sadly, some people are just pure evil. Regardless, people are always striving for perfection in some area of their lives. What if, however, Augustine is right and discovering our imperfections leads us to perfection? Is there an unbiased person who can point them out to us? Even if we can find one, how do we know that their opinion of perfection is right? God's word states that "people may be right in their own eyes, but the LORD examines their heart" (Proverbs 21:2 NLT). Since God can see what is inside someone's heart, He is probably the best one to point out and help us fix our imperfections.

Romans 12:2 (NIV) in the Bible says: "Do not conform to the pattern of this world but be transformed by the renewing of your mind. Then you will be able to test and approve what God's will is —his good, pleasing, and perfect will." So, if we ask God to show us our flaws and allow Him to transform our way of thinking, we will eventually learn what His will is for us. In addition, we can test and approve that will. The big difference between God's motives and the world's is that God's actions are motivated by His love for us. Did you know that 1 John 4:18 (NIV) states that His "perfect love drives out fear?" Plus, His power is made perfect in our weakness (2 Corinthians 12:9). You see the world is legalistic and judgmental, but God knows that we all sin and fall short of His glory (Romans 3:23). Therefore, we need to stop striving and acting like we are perfect people; instead, we need to ask God to show us our own imperfections and help us create a clean heart that is full of grace.

BATTLE PLAN: King David, the one who committed adultery and murder, was still a hero in the Bible and known as a man after God's own heart. King David said, "As for God, his way is perfect: the LORD'S word is flawless; he shields all who take refuge in him" (2 Samuel 22:31 NIV). When we find ourselves canceled by our culture and alone, we must remember that God will never leave us, and we are precious in His eyes. We cannot let the enemy succeed in making us worry about people's opinions of us, because God's opinion of us is all that really matters! Once we accept that we are not perfect and will never be perfect on this side of Heaven, we are free from the bondage of perfection. Our minds are no longer centered on us, and what others think of us, and the Lord can begin renewing the way we think about ourselves and others

BATTLE SONG: "Less Like Me" by Zach Williams

THE PARDON

"There is no pit so deep that He is not deeper still." —Corrie ten Boom

God gives mankind free will, so that they can do whatever they want to do. Unfortunately, some people use that gift for evil. The desire for power and money often leads to war and devastation. However, God will use even death and destruction to overcome evil with good. Christian writer Corrie Ten Boom's life was an example of this very thing, and her story is an inspiration for all of us. Her father, Casper, was a watchmaker who owned a jewelry shop in the Netherlands; Corrie worked in the shop as well. When the Nazis took control of the Netherlands, they started persecuting Jewish people. The Ten Boom family hid many Jews in a secret room on the top floor of their home for about a year before their operation was discovered.

One day, the secret police showed up at the Ten Boom's home and arrested the whole family. They also hid inside the house and arrested everyone that entered it. Casper died within a couple of weeks of captivity. Corrie and her sister, Betsie, were sent to Ravensbrück, which was one of the worst Nazi death camps. The women prisoners were beaten and overworked; some of them were used for medical experiments that led to their death, others died from starvation. The conditions were horrific, and Betsie eventually died. Corrie, however, did not give up and continued to put her faith in God. Perhaps she focused on Psalm 40:1-2 (NLT), because David said, "I waited patiently for the Lord to help me, and he turned to me and heard my cry. He lifted me out of the pit of despair, out of the mud and the mire. He set my feet on solid ground and steadied me as I walked along." God not only gets us out of the trenches, but he stabilizes us so that we can continue on our journey through life.

Shortly after Betsie died, Corrie was released from Ravensbrück. She traveled around Europe speaking about the importance of forgiving those who persecute us. She had the opportunity to practice what she preached, when a man in the audience approached her after her speech and told her that he was a former guard at Ravensbrück Who had become a Christian. He wanted her to personally tell him that she forgave him for his actions; Corrie told the man that he was forgiven. I believe that she was able to do this because she understood that we are all sinners saved by grace and we are called to forgive others if they repent from their evil ways and ask for forgiveness. Afterall, Jesus forgives us when we repent! David's pit in Psalm 40 was a metaphor for his despair; he could not seem to escape it. The takeaway from all of this is that when we suffer physical or mental anguish and cry out to God, He does hear us, and He will help us persevere until we are released of the suffering.

BATTLE PLAN: Doctors can bring physical healing from some injuries, but sometimes God is the only one who can bring mental healing from the trauma of war. Today, many of our veterans have lost their limbs, their hearing, and some of them physically suffer from Agent Orange, an herbicide that was used in Vietnam that causes nerve damage, while other suffer from the aftermath of the burn pits in Iraq and Afghanistan. God heard the cries of David and Corrie, and He will hear the cries of those injured from war. As for people like Casper and Betsie ten Boom, they received their rewards in Heaven when they arrived. God still had work for Corrie to do here: she showed the world how to forgive. When her mission was completed, she joined her family in Heaven. Corrie once said that "worry does not empty tomorrow of its sorrow, it empties today of its strength." When we wait and trust God, He will eventually bring good out of the bad (Romans 8:28). While we wait, we must not worry as it will rob us of the strength we need today to win the battle.

BATTLE SONG: "Forgiveness" by Matthew West

BATTLE SCARS

"The soldier above all others prays for peace, for it is the soldier who must suffer and bear the deepest wounds and scars of war." —Douglas MacArthur

Douglas MacArthur was a U.S. Army general who was instrumental in the victory of World War II, and saw the devastation that war brings. The phrase "time heals all wounds" is something we often say to someone, who is suffering physically or mentally from injury or loss, to bring them hope. Even when a physical wound is healed there is usually a physical scar that never goes away. Those who serve in the military refer to them as, "battle scars." Since God has a purpose for everything, what purpose do scars serve?

When Jesus was crucified, nails were driven through His hands and feet. Before He died, His side was pierced with a sword. The scars from His wounds played an important purpose after His resurrection—they proved who He was. One of His disciples, known as doubting Thomas, said, "Unless I see the nail marks in his hands and put my finger where the nails were, and put my hand into his side, I will not believe" that you saw Jesus (John 20:25 NIV). A week later, Jesus visited the disciples and Thomas did just what he said he was going to do.

When I was diagnosed with thyroid cancer, I had to have two surgeries. The surgeon made the incision for the second surgery where my scar was from the first surgery. As such, the scar across my throat would be even more visible than it was after the first operation. Some of my friends were telling me that I could get some scarves and wear them around my neck to hide the scar, but I did not feel the need to do that. Each time I looked at my battle scar it reminded me of God's faithfulness to heal me from cancer. Therefore, it reminded me who I was—a cancer survivor loved by God.

How we feel and speak about the scars we incur throughout life makes a difference in our attitude toward God and our future. Do we use them to bring glory to God, like Jesus did, or do we use them as an excuse to retreat from life? Sometimes people need to see our scars, like Thomas did, so that they are encouraged to continue on in the battle of life. With God's help, time can heal all wounds—if we let it.

BATTLE STRATEGY: Know your enemy! Satan is full of vanity, and he wants our focus to be on us and our lives so that we will be ineffective in the fight against evil. Jesus on the other hand, made himself of no reputation (Philippians 2:7). His goal wasn't to get people to esteem Him highly and worship Him. His mission of self-sacrifice was to save them from their sins. Jesus had several wounds, and it was His love for us that caused His scars. That love can also bring healing to our wounds so that through our testimony, we can bring healing to others.

BATTLE SONG: "Loving My Jesus" by Casting Crowns

I WILL RISE

"Do not rejoice over me, my enemy; when I fall, I will arise; when I sit in darkness, the Lord will be a light to me." —Micah 7:8 (NKJ)

There are many writings throughout the Bible about war. Although the enemies of the Jewish people in the Old Testament of the Bible and the apostles in the New Testament were often different, they had the same invisible leader behind them: Satan. Someone in the military has probably come face to face with this enemy on the battlefield—he has been around since the beginning of time. Micah was a prophet sent by God to warn the people that they needed to repent of their sinful ways or God would allow the Babylonians to conquer them. More importantly, he was to let the people know that God loved them but hated their sin. If they turned back to God, He would forgive and protect them. God could not continue to bless His children when they were dishonoring Him and His ways; anyone who is a parent can understand this concept. The setting during Micah's life was much like what is transpiring in America today. There was corruption, greed, oppression, division, sin, and hypocrisy. Evil was prevalent and people were fearful.

There are other reasons besides sin that can cause our enemy to succeed. Satan wants to keep us in bondage and some of his weapons are depression, addiction, and anxiety. I have experienced the effects of living with people afflicted with these wounds; it's heartbreaking to see them suffer because they fought sacrificially for the country they love. God understands how I feel because He watched Jesus suffer and die for the people He loves. Jesus, while on this earth, experienced the deep wounds that those who willingly sacrifice for others can incur, so He knows how they feel. That is why we need to cry out to Him for strength when we are struggling with wounds from the battlefield of life and trust in His ability to lead us to victory. It was Jesus' death and the light of salvation that overpowered the darkness of sin and illuminated the pathway to Heaven. Therefore, He is the one who can encourage us to arise and move forward.

BATTLE STRATEGY: President John F. Kennedy said, "We are not here to curse the darkness, but to light the candle that can guide us through that darkness to a safe and sane future." All our suffering is not in vain. It is during our darkest moments, when we cry out to the Lord, that He will be that light that helps us find our way through the darkness. Then we can proclaim the words in Micah 7:8 above to our enemy: "Do not rejoice over me, my enemy; when I fall, I will arise; when I sit in darkness, the Lord will be a light to me." Once we arise, we will be stronger than ever! Then, we can go on to light a candle that will help others find their way through the darkness to a bright future.

BATTLE SONG: "Our God" by Chris Tomlin

Navigating the Waves

Have you ever played in the waves when the surf was big? As a child, I was once described as a fish out of water because I loved being in the ocean. When a big wave was upon me, I would body surf it into the shore. However, sometimes I underestimated when an approaching wave would break. As such, I found myself at the mercy of the surf pulling me under the water and tossing me wherever it wanted. The more I played in the sea, the better I got at determining strategies to survive the unexpected break of a big swell. I discovered that the best way to escape the breaking crest that was suddenly upon me was to drop straight down under the water where it was calm. I would rise to the surface after the wave passed sometimes only to see another wave in front of me, which caused me to go back under the water.

One summer, a friend and her children went on vacation with me to North Carolina. Her kids had never really played in the waves and were a little afraid to try it, but once they were taught the secret of escaping the breaking whitecaps, you couldn't get them out of the water. Learning how to work with something they had no control over (the wave) freed them from the fear they had of it because they realized that they could take charge of their reaction to it.

There are many things in life that we cannot control; however, we can learn to navigate them safely and prevent them from overpowering us—the tempestuous sea of depression is one of those things. Once we succumb to despair it dominates us, like a breaking wave. We feel hopeless because we do not have the strength to fight its fierceness, leaving us at its mercy. Sometimes we can catch the gloom before it peaks and ride it into the shore of stability, but when life is sending one wave after another, we can easily become overwhelmed, unless we learn how to maneuver the surf. By taking control of the waves of hopelessness running through our minds and putting our focus on God's promise—that He is always with us—our emotions will not be tossed all over the place. Thus, allowing us to find His peace and calmness under the deep waters while we wait for what we cannot see.

BATTLE STRATEGY: Taking our thoughts captive should be the first response to the onset of depression. Romans 8:24-25 gives us one of the strategies we can use against the onslaught—HOPE. Preacher Charles Spurgeon said, "You will never know God's strength until he has supported you in deep waters." It is when the crest is breaking upon us that we need to go deep under the water and wait for the wave to pass. As we wait, we need to ask God to fill us with His breath of life and we will feel the calmness of His healing water. Each time we surface and face another swell, we will feel more confident because we have learned that diving deep into God's word will give us the strength and encouragement to persevere through the unpredictable waters around us!

BATTLE SONG: "Crashing Waves" by Michael W. Smith

THE HEALING FORGIVENESS BRINGS

"Forgive your enemies, but never forget their names." —John F. Kennedy

People who dedicate their lives for the good of others are fulfilling a purpose that is needed in the world. Soldiers fight enemies to protect the citizens of the country they live in; police officers protect the people of the cities they work in; and medical personnel help their patients keep their bodies free from viruses, bacteria, and injury. God created these selfless individuals with the gift of service. If their jobs were not necessary to accomplish the objective, why would they do them?

There are many people in the world today that believe that Jesus is the Son of God, however, they don't believe that He is the only way to Heaven. However, *if we can get into Heaven by being good, why did God send His Son to die for our sins?* My children are so precious to me, and I can't imagine watching them suffer and die in the place of others for no reason. God knows that we all sin because we are human, and we will until the day we die. Therefore, I'm sure that Jesus' sacrifice was the only way we could avoid Hell because someone has to pay for sin.

President Kennedy said that when we "forgive our enemies" we should remember their names. I am not quite sure what he meant by that, but my guess would be that when we forgive someone, we should never forget what they did. The problem with that theory is, how do you move on from the hurt and anger if you are still thinking about the offense? Even if you forget the incident, what happens when you hear the person's name; does everything resurface? It has been proven that holding grudges damages our mental and physical health. If this is true, who suffers from the unforgiveness more: the offender or the offended?

God says in His word that "as far as the east is from the west, so far has he removed our transgressions from us" (Psalm 103:12 NIV). When we repent of our sins, He not only forgives us—He erases the offense! In addition to that, the Lord remembers our name. "Can a woman forget her nursing child, and not have compassion on the son of her womb? Surely, they may forget, yet I will not forget you. See, I have inscribed you on the palms of my hands" (Isaiah 49:15-16 NKJ). When He remembers our name, He is not remembering our offenses from the past because they are gone—the slate is wiped clean!

Minister Martyn Lloyd-Jones once said, *"Whenever I see myself before God and realize something of what my blessed Lord has done for me at Calvary, I am ready to forgive anybody anything I cannot withhold it. I do not even want to withhold it."* Jones understood that if Jesus forgives us when we don't deserve it, then we need to forgive others when they don't deserve it. That is, however, easier said than done, but with God's help we can do it!

BATTLE PLAN: When we forgive others like the Lord tells us to do, we let God deal with those who offended us. He says, "I will take revenge; I will pay them back. In due time their feet will slip. Their day of disaster will arrive, and their destiny will overtake them" (Deuteronomy 32:35). God not only deals with our offender, but He also replaces the hurt and animosity inside us with love and peace. Can you see blessing? When we forgive others, WE are healed!

BATTLE SONG: "If We Only Knew" by Unspoken

LIFE IS A GIFT

"O Lord my God, I cried out to You, and You healed me. O Lord, You brought my soul up from the grave; You have kept me alive." —Psalm 30:2-3 (NKJ)

Why some people die and others live, is a question that many people have. My dad and my second husband, Glenn, died 3 weeks apart in June of 2009. My father had heart and kidney disease and was in his '80s; he really missed my mom, who died in 2005. As such, I felt that my dad lived a good life and was happy to be in Heaven with his wife. Glenn, on the other hand, was healthy and strong; he died of pancreatic cancer, four years after we were married—at the age of forty-five. I was the healthcare proxy for both of them and worked as a clinical instructor and lab teacher a few days a week. Being in the medical field, I just went into autopilot and physically did what came naturally. Emotionally, I sought God daily through His Word and if I was too tired to read, I watched a pastor on TV. A lot of people thought I would have a breakdown when they finally died, but I didn't. God was a solid rock for me to stand on and He always encouraged me.

Two years after Glenn and my dad died, I was diagnosed with ovarian cancer. I was scheduled to have surgery at a hospital that I used to work at, but my health insurance changed, and my doctor and the hospital were no longer an option for me. My doctor called an ovarian oncologist in Boston, who said he would take my case. When I went for an office visit, the doctor did more testing and he told me that I had to deal with my thyroid once I was done with my ovaries. I knew that in order for me to be healed I had to truly believe that God could and would heal me—I did believe He would heal me, and God gave me peace throughout the whole process.

I had surgery a week later and when the tumor was sent to pathology, it was benign. I asked the doctor if he could explain the results and he said no, it sometimes happens. I told him that God healed me. I did end up having cancer in my thyroid; however, it has been 10 years since then and I am cancer free. A couple of years ago when I was having an ultrasound to make sure my thyroid cancer had not come back, the radiologist told me that he had read my file and it was very interesting how they diagnosed my cancer. I asked him if he read all the test results for my ovaries that were in my file, and he said yes. I then said, *"looking at my tests, would you say that I had ovarian cancer?"* and he replied, *"Yes."* Throughout the Bible we read stories of miraculous healings. They are there to show us that all things are possible if we believe. What type of healing do you need today?

BATTLE PLAN: The Bible says that the day we die is written in God's book before we are even born (Psalm 139). So, when God healed my ovarian cancer, it wasn't my time to die and he saved me from going through chemo and radiation, which I am so grateful for! Former United States Secretary of State and Army General George C. Marshall said, "Military power wins battles, but spiritual power wins wars." We must realize that we are caught in a spiritual war and our best weapons are belief and prayer, so pray, pray, pray! We can't let the enemy win! When the enemy whispers in our ear, "You will never be healed" we must ask God to help us with any unbelief, then hold on to His promises in the Bible. God loves us and He will help us navigate through this season because He was the one who gave us the gift of life.

BATTLE SONG: "Healer" by Kari Jobe

THE MENDING OF A BROKEN HEART

"The harder the conflict, the more glorious the triumph." —Thomas Paine

The story of Joseph is written in the Old Testament of the Bible. He was the favorite son of a man named Jacob. Jacob loved him more than his other sons (Genesis 29, 30). Joseph's brothers were so jealous of him that they threw him in a pit. A caravan of men heading to Egypt was passing by and they sold Joseph to them as a slave, and then they told their father that Joseph was killed by an animal (Genesis 37).

When Joseph arrived in Egypt, he served his master, Potiphar, well and was put in charge of many things. However, Potiphar's wife lusted after Joseph. When Joseph refused her, she told everyone that Joseph had tried to seduce her (Genesis 39). Joseph was put in prison as a result, and although he was very good to the guards and inmates while serving his sentence, people took advantage of him and did not do the things they promised him they would do, so he remained in prison. The ruler of Egypt, Pharoah, had some troubling dreams and asked all the wisest men in Egypt what the dreams meant, but nobody knew. A chief butler who had been released from prison, told Pharoah about Joseph's ability to interpret dreams; Joseph was taken out of prison and brought to Pharoah. He interpreted Pharoah's dreams and told the great ruler that there would be seven years of abundant food and then seven years of great famine in the land; however, Joseph did not take credit for the wisdom he shared, he said it was his God who showed him these things. Pharoah said, "There is no one as discerning and wise as you. You shall be over my house and all my people shall be ruled according to your word" (Genesis 41:39-40 NKJ). God elevated Joseph because of his loyalty to Him.

The abundance of food from the first seven years was stored so when the famine hit, there was food for the people. When Jacob heard that there was food in Egypt, he sent his sons there to buy food. They were brought before Joseph and they did not recognize him, but

Joseph recognized them. Instead of punishing them for selling him into slavery, he chose to forgive them, saying, "I am Joseph your brother, whom you sold into Egypt. But don't be upset, and don't be angry with yourselves for selling me to the place. It was God who sent me here ahead of you to reserve your lives...to keep your families alive and to preserve many survivors. So, it was God who sent me here not you! (Genesis 45:4-8 NLT). Through the false accusations, imprisonment, and suffering Joseph endured, a nation was saved, and his broken heart was mended. Joseph's healing came because he could see that all the events that occurred in his life happened so that Egypt, as well as his family, could survive the famine. If you have been betrayed or abandoned, don't lose heart; God can work things together for good (Romans 8:28).

BATTLE PLAN: Suffering is never in vain when good comes out of it. There were many great things that came from the horrific events of 9/11 in America. Stephen Sillers was an off-duty firefighter who ran to the Twin Towers to help and lost his life. His brother Frank developed an organization called Tunnel to Towers that pays off mortgages and builds houses for the families of those who gave their life in the line of duty and for veterans and first responders who are badly injured. Jesus suffered terribly through His crucifixion, however, His death opened the door for us to go to Heaven when we die. God always brings good out of bad and has a purpose for allowing our suffering. If you are enduring tremendous loss or pain right now, pray for God to help you through it, remain faithful, and someday you will see the good that came from it.

BATTLE SONG: "There was Jesus" by Zach Williams & Dolly Parton

PRIDE CAN HINDER HEALING

"It is an invariable maxim in his kingdom, that whosoever exalts himself, shall be abased; but he that humbles himself, shall be exalted." —John Newton

The old adage "God helps those who help themselves" was a popular phrase when I was growing up. It was often used when people were elevating their status or being selfish. Although I never understood this idiom as a child, I realized that there was some truth to this saying when I got older and read the Old Testament of the Bible.

In the book of 2 Kings verse 5, there is a story about a man named Naaman who had leprosy. Since he was the commander of the Syrian army, it is believed that Naaman had only a mild case of leprosy. He would often attack Israel, and during one of his raids he took a young Israeli girl captive and brought her to his house. The girl told Naaman's wife that the prophet Elisha might be able to heal her husband, so Naaman went to see Elisha. The prophet instructed him to "go wash in the Jordan seven times, and your flesh shall be restored to you, and you shall be clean" (2 Kings 5:10 NKJ). Naaman was insulted that he wasn't treated as the great man he thought he was and left in anger. He had his own vision of how his healing would take place; it would be something miraculous. Washing in a river that was not that clean was unacceptable to him. In fact, there were other rivers much cleaner than the Jordan. Naaman finally realized that he had no other options for his healing, so he let go of his pride and did exactly what he was told to do, and he was healed of his leprosy.

We may think that Naaman's reaction to the instruction for healing was childish, but how many times do we do similar things? Maybe we were proven wrong in a situation, but our pride wouldn't let us admit that the other person was right. Then, when we finally admitted we were wrong we leave without apologizing. The story of Naaman shows us that even when God heals us, he is more concerned with the state of our heart than the physical ailment we have. I believe this is because a physical disability will not keep us out of Heaven, whereas unrepentance can. One of my friends had a terminal cancer called leiomyosarcoma and she had a year to live. She believed that

God could heal her, but he wasn't healing her. One day, He showed her while she was praying that she had unforgiveness toward some people. She immediately asked God for forgiveness and forgave those people. She had tests a week later and her tumor had disintegrated, all that was there was the sack the tumor was in, and the cells in the sack were not even cancerous.

When we find ourselves in a situation that is hopeless, we need to evaluate our heart and our attitude to see if there is any sin hindering the answer to our prayers. John 15:2 NLT says, "He cuts off every branch of mine that doesn't produce fruit, and he prunes the branches that do bear fruit so they will produce even more." As God cuts off our branches of pride, unforgiveness, or unbelief, we will grow stronger and become healthy, which enables to be useful in the battle.

BATTLE STRATEGY: Satan was thrown out of Heaven because of his pride. He convinced some angels that he was equal or even more powerful than God, so they followed him. His tactics never change. Therefore, he will try to convince us that our opinions, knowledge, or status is better than others. Once he gets us to this point, God takes a step back from empowering us or using us. When we have the urge to compare ourselves with others, the first person we should start with is Jesus—we will be reminded that pride was not one of His characteristics.

BATTLE SONG: "Lay Down My Pride" by Jeremy Camp

A TIME TO BREAK DOWN, AND
A TIME TO BUILD UP
—ECCLESIASTES 3:3B

Building Up Faith

"He got into a boat and His disciples followed Him. And suddenly a great tempest arose on the sea, so that the boat was covered with the waves. But He was asleep. Then His disciples came to Him and awoke Him, saying 'Lord, save us! We are perishing!' But He said to them, 'why are you fearful, O you of little faith?' Then He arose and rebuked the winds and the sea, and there was a great calm." —
Matthew 8:23-26 (NKJ)

As I write this I am sitting on a deck above the sand, on a beach in Florida. The hot tropical breeze is continuous, and the swells are big. There is a group of people kite surfing in the ocean in front of me. Each person is holding onto a sail-like parachute, while their feet are attached to a small surf type board. Some of the people are letting the wind carry them as they glide across the top of the sea, while a couple of people intentionally turn into the large swells, which jets them high into the air. Their landing back on the water's surface must be precise, if not, they can land in the surf and fall beneath the water and their feet will dislodge from the board. I enjoyed surfing when I was a teenager and I understand what a wipeout in the waves can do to you. I cannot imagine how difficult it would be to hold onto the bar of the parachute while being tossed around by waves and currents. When I did not have faith in my ability to surf, I often got pummeled by the waves; however, when I followed my instincts and trusted what I knew, I was more successful. Believing in ourselves to accomplish things can be difficult because doubt and fear can easily creep in; however, believing in God's ability within us is another story.

The disciples witnessed Jesus' power when He calmed the storm; yet there were times when they doubted their ability to do what He said they could do. "Jesus called His twelve disciples to him and gave them authority to drive out impure spirits and to heal every disease and sickness" (Matthew 10:1 NIV) then He sent them out. However, a man brought his epileptic son to the disciples to be healed, but they couldn't heal him. When the man saw Jesus and told Him the story, Jesus healed the boy. The disciples asked Jesus why they could not heal him, and Jesus told them it was because of their unbelief (Matthew 17:20). Minister Christmas Evans said, "Faith is not a sense, nor sight, nor reason, but simply taking God at His word." Soldiers in a battle believe what their commanding officer tells them. Therefore, when they are fully equipped for a mission, they move out with confidence. Similarly, we must *believe* God's promises and Jesus' words in the Bible. When we do, we can overcome the powerful gusts of fear and the waves of depression by denouncing their power over us and moving forward.

BATTLE PLAN: People in the armed forces use their weapons to defeat the attacking enemy; their shots must be precise. Likewise, we need to use the word of the Lord to defeat the devil. When I was a child, the kids in my neighborhood had a saying when they were being bullied: "Sticks and stones will break my bones, but names will never hurt me." Proclaiming that phrase gave us power over the threatening words that were hurled at us. We let the bullies know that they were not effective in accomplishing their verbal assault. Proclaiming God's word to Satan stops him in his tracks and gives you power over him, so remember this when he is penetrating your thoughts—counter his lies with God's truths. Through life we can play it safe and glide across the sea, hoping we do not get overpowered by the waves, or we can choose to take them on and experience all God has planned for us. Let us put our faith in God and secure a victory!

BATTLE SONG: "Same Power" by Jeremy Camp

It's Not What You Know, It's Who You Know

"If you wish to know God, you must know His word. If you wish to perceive His power, you must see how He works by his word. If you wish to know His purpose before it comes to pass, you can only discover it by His word." —*Charles Spurgeon*

Jesus' purpose for leaving Heaven and coming to Earth was not only to die for our sins so that we could gain eternal life, but to also teach people who His Father is. Jesus said, "Now this is eternal life that they know you, the only true God, and Jesus Christ, whom you have sent" (John 17:3 NIV). When a mother gives birth, her purpose is to bring a child into the world, but her job doesn't end there; as her baby grows, she begins to teach, nurture, comfort, discipline, encourage, and love her child. As their relationship grows, a bond of trust is formed and even when they are separated, the mother's words remain in the child's mind and heart.

I think it is safe to say that for a child to have a relationship with a parent, they need to spend time with them. When Christ was born, He grew up in a typical Jewish home. His earthly parents taught and cared for Him; when He got older, He began His life's mission. As He traveled throughout the countryside, He talked about His heavenly Father and taught the people His ways. Prior to that, the people had no idea how God really felt about them or things in general. In the Old Testament there were prophets that God spoke through, but they were mere men, and some people did not take their warnings seriously. Today, we are blessed to have God's written word in the Bible. When we read the New Testament, Jesus' words speak volumes to us; every answer we need in life is written in this book. When we face a devasting diagnosis or lose a loved one, the written words in the Bible come to life and touch our heart and soul. They speak words of love, hope, comfort, and healing. Therefore, it's important to know God's word.

Some people contact me when they need prayer for a serious problem; they say I have a direct link to God—I believe I do! In fact, everyone can have that connection with Him as well; as with any relationship, it grows and flourishes as we get to know one another. It is when we put our effort and time into knowing somebody that we begin to build trust, respect, and love for them. Putting in the effort to build a personal relationship with the Lord was the best thing that I ever did for myself! If you haven't made the effort to know the Lord, why not do it today—you have nothing to lose and everything to gain.

BATTLE PLAN: The Apostle Peter said, "Lord to whom shall we go? Thou hast the words of eternal life" (John 6:68 KJV). Just as the apostles learned firsthand from Jesus' words, so can we—the only thing that is preventing us from truly knowing God is us! In a world full of chaos, it is paramount that we build a strong relationship with Him, so that He can guide, encourage, and protect us. Since none of us know the future, why not get to know the one who has all the answers? Beware, the enemy of your soul will do everything to keep you from knowing God intimately; therefore, watch out for his attacks and don't let him be successful!

BATTLE SONG: "Your Words" by Third Day

Building Barricades

"Your personal boundaries protect the inner core of your identity and your right to choices." —Gerard Manley Hopkins

Barricades are built for many different reasons: to shield, to enclose, to section off, and to protect. Some of these structures are temporary while others are permanent. It only makes sense that we would want to block anything harmful from reaching us or those we love. One area we often forget to build a barrier around is our mind. Nowadays, more than ever it's essential that we protect ourselves from the abundance of information on social media. It appears that some people have lost their sense of integrity, compassion, and desire for the truth. Many parents put blocks on their TV's and other technology so that their children cannot access inappropriate content. However, adults do not realize that they need protection from certain material as well. With physical boundaries we determine if something is good or bad before we allow access through the barricade, so why don't we do that with our minds?

I heard a story once that I shared with my kids when they wanted to compromise a little on their morals; perhaps you have heard this story as well: A dad was making homemade cookies with his kids and told them that he had a little bit of dog poop that he was going to add to the batter. The children were horrified and said, "You can't put that in the cookies." The dad said, "why not, it's only a little bit and you probably won't even be able to taste it." The father did not have to explain anything else to his children because they totally understood that just a little compromise can make a big difference.

The apostle Peter gave a warning: "Be sober, be vigilant; because your adversary the devil walks about like a roaring lion, seeking whom he may devour" (1 Peter 5:8 KJV). Satan is relentless and is always searching for the tiniest opening in the fence of our integrity or judgment. Sometimes, all it takes is for us to have a weak moment and we compromise and let the enemy in. Once he penetrates our thoughts, he can persuade us to do things we ordinarily wouldn't do. He has been doing since the beginning of time; he convinced Eve to eat the forbidden fruit in the Garden of Eden. Therefore, we must be vigilant about protecting the boundaries of our mind.

BATTLE PLAN: To have a strong barricade we need to frequently assess the structure for any weak areas that the enemy can breach. We should also have an alarm system that signals when something threatening is trying to enter our area. If we are outside our protected area, we should have a warning system that will alert our mind that temptation is around the corner, and we should take an alternate route. Never underestimate your enemy's ability to lure you in "For Satan himself masquerades as an angel of light" (2 Corinthians 11:14 NIV). As such, not everything that looks good or everyone that looks safe to enter our protected area is. Remember the dad with the tiny bit of dog poop, it only takes a little sin to spoil our marriage, our reputation, or our integrity. If we do fall for one of the enemies' traps, we must repent and ask God to forgive us and help us make good decisions and strong barriers. He will not only forgive us, but He will also help us rebuild our barricade, which will be stronger than ever!! He can help us rebuild whatever sin has destroyed.

BATTLE SONG: "Strong Tower" by Kutless

BUILDING UP OTHERS

"You dear friends must build each other up in your most holy faith, pray in the power of the Holy Spirit, and await the mercy of our Lord Jesus Christ, who will bring eternal life. In this way, you will keep yourselves safe in God's love." —Jude 1:20 (NLT)

The above scripture was written by Jesus' brother Jude. Before Jude gave that message to his fellow Christians, he warned them that there would be skeptics and unbelievers in the last days. "These people are the ones who are creating divisions among you. They follow their natural instincts because they do not have God's Spirit in them" (Jude 1:19 NLT). Sounds a lot like what is going on in the world today; there is not only political party divisions but also separation between the COVID vaccinated and unvaccinated. Even Christians are divided in these areas, as well as the abortion laws.

People who have not read the Old Testament of the Bible might think these issues and divisions never happened before in history, but they have they were just named differently: abortion was called child sacrifice; the political parties were the Jews and the Christians; and the vaccine for leprosy was Jesus who miraculously healed lepers. Jude said to persevere through tumultuous times we must, "show mercy to those whose faith is wavering. Rescue others by snatching them from the flames of judgement. Show mercy still to others but do so with great caution hating the sins that contaminate their lives" (Jude 1:22-23 NLT). We all sin, therefore, we cannot be too quick to judge others. It is when we compare ourselves to Jesus and not each other that we are reminded of how imperfect we are. Military teams encourage and build each other up, especially when they have experienced something a comrade is going through. They are not in a competition against one another, and they are able to put their personal differences aside and fight together for a common goal. Civilian life should be the same, so let's encourage and support one another, so we can fight and win the battles that we encounter in our daily lives.

BATTLE PAN: Former US Army general Norman Schwarzkopf Jr. said, "the truth of the matter is that you always know the right thing to do. The hard part is doing it." Soldiers get the job done; they don't put things off until tomorrow because they may lose the upper hand they have on their enemy. They also know that there is strength in numbers, especially in a battle because enemies will always attack the weakest unit. These strategies work for all people in every profession. Therefore, we must build each other up. We need to rescue a brother/sister when they're alone and helpless. If they have turned away from God and their faith, we can show mercy and remind them of God's grace and forgiveness. If we are unable to meet with people in person, we can call them and encourage them. We can also provide supporting fire by praying when they are under attack, which invites God to join us in our mission. Prayer has been known to move mountains if the person praying has faith the size of a mustard seed (Matthew 17:20). If we are the ones who need direct support, we need to let people know that we are struggling, so they can provide us with tactical knowledge and help us develop a strategic battle plan and security measures. Activist Mahatma Gandhi once said, "The best way to find yourself is to lose yourself in the service of others." Let's evaluate ourselves, realize our weaknesses, and come together and fight the enemy of our soul and not each other. With God by our side, we can't lose!

BATTLE SONG: "Give Me Your Eyes" by Brandon Heath

BUILDING UP WISDOM

"Wisdom is the right use of knowledge. To know is not to be wise. Many men know a great deal and are all the greater fools for it. There is no fool so great a fool as a knowing fool. But to know how to use knowledge is to have wisdom." — Charles Spurgeon

There are many old adages that have some truth to them; here are a few that you may agree with: "Birds of a feather flock together," "the truth hurts," and "misery loves company." When someone is miserable, they often get aggravated when a person tries to cheer them up. They would rather be around somebody that will agree with their attitude and fuel their fire. Perhaps being around a happy person makes them envious or just intensifies their unhappiness. As such, going out with a drinking buddy, or going on a shopping spree with their BFF might be how they deal with their emotions. This, however, is only a temporary fix that might add to their problem, rather than solve it, especially if they get caught drunk driving, or spend money they do not have. Denial of our situation will never solve our problems and to rise above them, we need to first accept where we are. If we find that we are flying with a flock that is going in the wrong direction, we need to find a new one to travel with. Even though the truth hurts, we often need to hear it.

To get out of the pit of despair, we need encouragement, not justification to stay there. When we choose to remain in despair, we are often fulfilling the description of insanity: "doing the same thing over and over again but expecting different results." The apostle Paul said, "For what I am doing, I do not understand, for what I will to do, that I do not practice; but what I hate, that I do" (Romans 7:15 NKJ). Many of us realize that there is a war between good and evil in the world, but don't realize that there is an internal battle raging between our spirt and our flesh The apostle Paul concluded that he was a wretched man who needed someone to rescue him (Romans 7:24), which Jesus did. Sometimes, God uses people to rescue those who are losing their internal battle. Therefore, seeking the wisdom of others who have successfully overcome the same problem we are experiencing can be very helpful. Soldiers who have conquered an enemy can always help a different squad achieve the same outcome. We need to ask ourselves today, are we wise, or are we *"a knowing fool?"*

BATTLE PLAN: Spurgeon said in the opening quote that a person needs knowledge to be wise, but also must *use* that knowledge. God has given us a precious book full of hope, encouragement, and guidance with examples of those who have successfully gone before us. Hebrews 11 is all about people who trusted and obeyed what God was calling them to do, and He filled them with wisdom and strength. Against all odds, battles were won and people were healed. These stories were written in the Bible to encourage us. If, however, we choose to be foolish and wise in our own eyes, then we will remain in the captivity of depression and Satan will be the victor. Yet, if we choose to seek the help of God and others, we begin the journey out of despair, and we can be victorious!

BATTLE SONG: God of All My Days by Casting Crowns

BUILDING CONFIDENCE

"I am sending you to Pharaoh to bring my people the Israelites out of Egypt. But Moses said to God, who am I that I should go to Pharaoh." —Exodus 3:10-11 (NIV)

Some of us learned about the story of Moses by watching the 1956 epic film *The Ten Commandments*. If you recall, he was a Jewish baby, decreed to be killed. His mom put him in a waterproof basket and put the basket in the reeds on the bank of the Nile River (Exodus 2:3 NIV). When Pharaoh's daughter went to the river, she found Moses and she ended up raising him as her son. He grew up as royalty, but then fled the kingdom when he murdered someone. Many years later, God told Moses to go to Pharaoh and tell him to free the Jews who were being held in captivity. God saved Moses from death when he was a baby for this very purpose.

Exodus verses 10-11 states that Moses replied to God "Who am I." because he did not feel qualified for the job. I imagine he had mixed emotions about the type of man he was. Even though Moses was defending an innocent man when he killed the man's attacker, his life was now chaotic, his identity changed, and he had no idea who he was. That sometimes happens to us when we decide to get involved in a situation to help someone; we are suddenly dragged into a battle that we wanted no part of.

Evangelist Oswald Chambers said, "Beware of harking back to what you once were when God wants you to be something you have never been." Even if Moses wanted to go back to being a member of Pharaoh's family, he couldn't. God had bigger plans for him: leading the Israelites to the promised land. When Moses did approach Pharaoh regarding the release of the people, God gave Moses everything he needed to accomplish the task. When Moses held up his staff the Red Sea parted, and the Israelites were able to escape Pharaoh's army that was closing in on them. Through Moses, God performed amazing miracles and God is still doing that today through ordinary people who have surrendered their lives to Him. Sometimes when our life seems like it is at the very worst point that it could ever be, it might be because we are trying to retreat instead of moving forward toward who we were created to be.

BATTLE PLAN: If you find yourself in a place today where your world is torn upside down, do not fear. As C.S. Lewis said, "Hardship often prepares an ordinary person for an extraordinary destiny." God has a purpose for your life, just as He did for Moses. Spend time with Him and listen for His guidance. When you get the call to move, don't be afraid to step out into the wilderness because God will be beside you all the way. He will accomplish amazing things through you!

BATTLE SONG: "Finding Who We Are" by Kutless

BREAK DOWN THE STRONGHOLDS

"We are human, but we don't wage war as humans do. We use God's mighty weapons, not worldly weapons, to knock down the strongholds of human reasoning and to destroy false arguments."— 2 Corinthians 10:3-4(NLT)

My dad served in the navy during World War II on the USS Bennington Aircraft Carrier. The ship provided cover for US troops fighting on the Japanese islands, and also sent fighter planes to destroy the strongholds in Okinawa and the surrounding islands. The American pilots bombed airfields and dodged gunfire from the Japanese navy.

My brothers and I would ask my dad about the war, but he never wanted to talk about it. My older cousin would tell us a story about the samurai sword that my dad gave him when he came home from the war. The only story I remember my dad telling me was about the time he got off the Bennington in Japan when the war ended. He had a chocolate bar in his pocket and tried to give it to a 5-year-old Japanese boy, who spit at him. My father loved kids and I know his heart was broken when that happened because of the sadness in his eyes when he told me the story. The boy had no idea that Japan bombed Pearl Harbor before they even declared war against the United States—leaving many Americans dead. All the boy knew was the destruction that America caused to his country. Territory that is fought over in a war eventually gets conquered and the war ends; however, the battlefield of the mind lives on long after the war is over. The mental and emotional effects suffered by those who served in the military during World War II was labeled "shellshock." My father occasionally had bad dreams about the war until the day he died. One morning he came downstairs with cuts on his head and arms, having gone to bed fine. I asked him, "where did you get those cuts?!" He answered, "I had a dream that I was on the Bennington and a kamikaze was dive bombing us, so I dove off the ship into the water." The dream seemed so real to my dad that he actually dove out of his bed into the radiator next time him, causing the injuries.

Not even those in the highest ranks can 100% control the events that take place during a war. Yet, there is something that everyone can control and that is their mind: by taking their thoughts captive and not revisiting the past. Marcus Aurelius was a Roman emperor who once said, "You have power over your mind—not outside events. Realize this, and you will find strength." That seems like a good concept to put into action, so why is it so hard for people to do it? It is because the enemy of our soul never wants us to forget the hurt and destruction we witnessed. He wants to keep us captive, like prisoners who see the open cell door but are afraid to venture out into the unknown. One way of doing this is to convince us to keep our feelings to ourselves. When we don't talk about things, they often show up in our dreams and we relive events. When we bring God into the situation, He can help us win the battle in our minds.

BATTLE PLAN: God has given us the ammunition to fight Satan, but we must believe that His word is more powerful than the enemy's lies. The devil may whisper in our ear that we shouldn't talk about our ailments; this is because he wants to keep us in bondage. My dad never sought help for his "shellshock." Perhaps if he had talked about what he was feeling, the dreams would have stopped. God sometimes sends healing through doctors, and other times it is through miracles. If we seek God for guidance, He will strengthen us and lead us to the path of healing and peace.

BATTLE SONG: "Hold Me Jesus" by Big Daddy Weave

BREAKING DOWN THE DAMS WE BUILD

"It is life, I think to watch the water. A man can learn so many things." —
Nicholas Sparks

Water generally flows freely, and it usually finds a way to overcome obstacles by sneaking through the tiniest cracks and crevasses. However during a drought, a mighty river may dwindle down to a few puddles. Sometimes the flow of a body of water is stopped by a dam that beavers have built. Although beavers do not live in the dams they construct, they build them to create deeper pools of water to protect their homes from their predators. Centuries ago, people built moats around their homes. These deep ditches filled with water were used as a barrier to protect the homeowner from enemies, as well.

Did you know that water in the bible represents the Holy Spirit? Just like deep pools of water protect the beavers and moats protected people, the Holy Spirit can keep us safe by guiding us and making us aware of our enemy. It is during our most difficult times when it appears that all our waterways are blocked or dried up that God leaves a little puddle of hope to remind us that all is not lost. If we do not give up and have faith in God, He can "make the wilderness a pool of water" (Isaiah 41:18 KJV) and His Holy Spirit is looking for the smallest crack to seep into our lives to fill us with hope and peace. Unfortunately, sometimes we build a dam of disbelief that prevents the living waters of His Spirit to flow through the river of our lives. Instead, we try all kinds of worldly methods to gain peace and healing that don't work.

The opening quote says "it is life…to watch the water because we can learn so much." Likewise, by watching the lives of people who are filled with the Holy Spirit, we learn about God. My neighbor watched me bury my dad and husband three weeks apart. Two years later, I was diagnosed with ovarian cancer. By praying and reading God's word daily, He was able to encourage me and remind me that He loves me, and He is in control. God came through for me during all kinds of trials. Therefore, when I was diagnosed with cancer, I knew that God would get me through that season of my life, and He did! I even had peace during the process. After my surgery, I was walking my dog and my neighbor asked me if I could come in her house for a minute, so I did. She said that she was expecting me to have a nervous breakdown when I got the cancer diagnosis, but I hadn't. The crazy thing is, I had no idea that she was watching my life so closely and how I reacted to the circumstances I encountered. It was by watching the water of the Holy Spirit flow through my life that my neighbor accepted Jesus, as her Lord and Savior. God has a plan for our suffering, and He will help us through it. Our job is to breakdown the dam of unbelief that we have built and let God's living waters create deep pools of trust and faith.

BATTLE PLAN: The Dead Sea has no marine life in it; there is a waterway that flows into it, but no waterway that flows out. Therefore, it does create a deep pool; however, the salt content is so high that no living thing can survive it. When we find that our spirit is dead from the abundance of bitter salt, we can choose to empty our souls of the tainted water and let the Holy Spirit fill us with living waters. Once our pool is full of life, faith and peace, the water flowing freely through us can bring hope and encouragement to those who are experiencing a drought. Beavers don't build dams to keep the water *out* of their life, but rather to create a deep pool of water for protection. Our deep pool of healing water can protect us from the devil's torpedoes of despair. Then, we'll be able to overcome any obstacles in our path because that's what water does!

BATTLE SONG: "Living Waters" by Keith & Kristyn Getty

Build Up Your Faith & Stamina

"If all of life were sunshine,
Our face would long to gain
And feel once more upon it
The cooling splash of rain"
—Henry Jackson Van Dyke

People in the military often have to trek through very difficult terrain. They cross deserts, bodies of water, and sometimes dense forests. In addition to the weather and the landscape, they carry a rucksack filled with provisions, extra clothes, tactical and survival gear (that can weigh up to 50 pounds), and possibly a radio. Stamina is built during Boot Camp, but their training does not end when they complete the program; physical training is a daily ritual. When they are not in combat, the do field exercises and participate in scheduled training events. They are always building stamina and are prepared to go to battle. Do you know that God often uses similar techniques to build up our endurance, too?

Sometimes we think that God is punishing us when we are hit with one of life's bad storms out of nowhere. The gale force winds make it difficult for us to hold onto our backpacks we've filled with peace, faith, and hope. Even though God has trained us through past experiences, sometimes the elements are too powerful for us to fight alone, so we might take shelter in a dense forest. However, once the rain and wind pass, we then can't find our way out of the woods; or perhaps we could navigate the terrain, but we are too afraid to go back out into the open meadow, so we make a shelter in the forest instead. It is during times like this that God often allows situations that push us out of our protective area into the grasslands because He knows we need the sunshine (and the rain) to survive. But then, all of a sudden we start encountering bears and wolves, so we flee the woods and return to the shelter we had set up when the storm hit.

Similarly, when we have experienced the whirlwind of betrayal, the monsoon of heartbreak, or the cloudburst of injury, we often choose to retreat from life and stay in the house where we feel safe. However, when we stop interacting with others and become a recluse,

God will send something to push us out. He knows if we stay withdrawn from society the wolves of depression and the bear of anxiety will begin to attack us. Therefore, we must fight the desire to stay isolated from God and people, and venture out into the open field where we can feel the sun and the healing rain that brings life.

BATTLE PLAN: Military commanders do everything in their power to rescue their soldiers when they are in danger. They will send planes to fire heavy artillery at the enemy and helicopters to land, so the soldiers have a way to leave the danger and return to their base. It would be crazy for one of them to refuse the help and not board the helicopter. Unfortunately, we do not look at depression or anxiety as imminent danger and often refuse the help our heavenly commander is sending us. The biggest problems causing our resistance are denial and pride. The enemy knows this, so he will make sure he provides us with opportunities to act out these attributes. After all, his goal is to wear us down, so he can keep us in bondage and torment us. Therefore, we must stay in constant contact with God through praying and reading His word, so He can tell us how to escape while we can. Once we do escape, we will look back and realize that what Satan meant for harm, God used to build our stamina and bring us closer to Him.

BATTLE SONG: "Heaven Help" Me by Zach Williams

A TIME TO WEEP, AND A TIME TO LAUGH—ECCLESIASTES 3:4A

TURNING TEARS TO PRAISE

"Day and night I have only tears for food, while my enemies continually taunt me, saying 'Where is this God of yours?'" —Psalm 42:3 (NLT)

David wrote this psalm while he was fleeing from King Saul and struggling with depression. He cries out to God in verses one and two saying, "As the deer longs for streams of water, so I long for you, O God. I thirst for God, the living God. When can I go and stand before him?" David's soul was longing to be with God; he was tired of fighting his enemies—his mind was troubled. In verse 5 of Psalm 42 David encouraged himself, "Why am I discouraged? Why is my heart so sad? I will put my hope in God! I will praise him again." David not only took his thoughts captive, but he also came up with a battle plan.

We often find ourselves in the same predicament that David was in, and we may even feel that we want to go be with God. It was through surrendering his deepest wounds to God that David was free of them. His tears turned to praise as he remembered how faithful God had been to rescue him in the past. We can all learn a lesson from David's example—instead of complaining to God about his situation, he began confessing the pain in his heart and soul. When depression is consuming us, we must cry out to God and let him know about the pain we are feeling, rather than blaming Him for our dilemma.

BATTLE PLAN: Remember, Jesus said that Satan is the father of lies (John 8:44). Once we realize this and recognize Satan's tactics, we are able to counter them with God's promises of abundant life. When the devil is flooding our minds with memories of the past, and hurling accusations against us saying, *'Where is this God of yours?'*—we need to remember the times that God came through for us. This reflection will give us hope and allow us to rise above the attacks from the enemy; we can go from feeling hopeless to feeling grateful, just like David did. As we feel the healing begin, we not only start becoming the people we were before the war began, but we are a wiser and stronger version of ourselves!

BATTLE SONG: "Tell Your Heart to Beat Again" by Danny Gokey

TIME IS RUNNING OUT

"The Lord says, 'Turn to me now, while there is time. Give me your hearts. Come with fasting, weeping, and mourning." —Joel 2:12 (NLT)

As I write this Russia is attacking Ukraine. Many Ukrainians are fleeing the country to find safety in neighboring countries. Meanwhile, the male citizens 18 years or older are staying in Ukraine to defend their land and freedom. Some of the Ukrainians left the country when there were just rumors of war, while others did not, and they are now frantically trying to find a way out of the warzone. Why is it that we always think we have more time than we really do?

In 1964, a musical group called the Rolling Stones made a record titled, "Time is on My Side." The song is about a guy and his girlfriend; the girl wanted her freedom, so that she could have fun and he set her free. He knew that she would eventually come running back to him and he would take her back because he truly loved her. Do you know that God feels the same way about us? His love, however, is stronger than any type of earthly love. "He is gracious and merciful, slow to anger and of great kindness" (Joel 2:13 KJV). He gives His children plenty of warning to turn from their sinful ways because He wants to bless them, not punish them. You see, time is on God's side. We never know which day will be our last day on earth, but He does. Therefore, it's paramount for us to always be in good standing with Him.

The title of the Book of Joel in the New King James Version of the Bible is called, "The Day of the Lord." Joel was one of God's prophets and he was sent to warn the nation of Judah (the Southern Kingdom) that judgement would come to them if they did not repent of their sinful ways. The people had become self-sufficient and self-righteous because God's favor was on them, and He allowed them to prosper. There is nothing wrong with being wealthy as long as we remember that everything we have comes from God. My second husband always said that we had what we had because we worked hard to get it. I would say, no it's because God is pouring His blessings on us. Unfortunately, it wasn't until my husband was diagnosed with inoperable pancreatic cancer that he realized that God had blessed him in the past with good health, so he could work—meaning we had everything we had because God blessed us. Sadly, it often takes disease, unemployment, or sometimes missile launches to get us to communicate with our heavenly Father. The old military adage "There are no atheists in foxholes" means that people, who don't believe that God exists, tend to pray to Him for help when they are possibly facing death. If they do humble themselves and repent, God will hear their prayers. Another anomaly is that people who are not even Christians are noticing that the end-times prophecies in the Bible are coming true. Therefore, the rapture could happen at any time, and it will happen in a blink of an eye. If we blink our eye right now, we will see that there isn't even time to get one word out of our mouths. Why take a chance on being left behind and going through hell on earth while there is still time to escape it!

BATTLE STRATEGY: Satan loves to see people who are self-sufficient and living the "good life," because they believe that they are in control of everything and have no need of a savior; however, their prestige and money will not get them into Heaven. Therefore, trials are a good thing if they lead us back to God. He loves us more than the boyfriend in the Rolling Stones song, and He is always waiting to take us back! The question is, will we run back to Him in time?

BATTLE SONG: "Never Too Far Gone" by Jordan Feliz

WEEPING TEARS OF ETERNAL LIFE

*"The flowers live by the tears that fall
From the sad face of the skies;
And life would have no joys at all,
Were there no watery eyes.
Love thou thy sorrow: grief shall bring
Its own excuse in after years;
The rainbow! —see how fair a thing
God hath built up from tears."*
—Henry S. Sutton

Most people have good intentions but severely underestimate their ability to practice what they preach. It's so easy for us to say, "I would never do that!" My mom taught me at any early age to "never say the word never, because you don't know how you will act in a situation until it happens." The Bible says that "Pride goes before destruction and haughty spirit before a fall" (Proverbs16:18 NIV), and many of us have discovered the truth in that scripture.

Jesus told Peter "This very night, before the rooster crows, you will deny three times that you even know me" (Matthew 26:34 NLT). The Apostle Peter replied, "Even if I have to die with you, I will never deny you!" (Matthew 26:35 NLT). However, after he denied knowing Christ three times because he feared death, the rooster crowed three times and Peter *wept bitterly* (Matthew 26:69-75). I believe that God allowed Peter to learn the "never say never lesson" for many reasons: to not think more highly of himself than he actually was; to realize that the spirit is willing, but the flesh is weak; and that even when he fails, Jesus still loves him and will use his shortcomings for God's kingdom.

It was through Peter's *tears and sorrow* that he became so successful in spreading the gospel—he understood the meaning of grace, forgiveness, and restoration. Peter never lived to see all the fruit from his labor: God built His church on Peter's testimony of Jesus, just like Christ predicated. God knows that "our righteous acts are like filthy rags" (Isaiah 64:6 NIV) and it is only when we realize this, that He can use our lives to do great things for His kingdom.

So where do we find ourselves today on our journey in life? Are we self-sufficient and think that we will never go back on our word? If so, we need to beware; perhaps we have never faced a gruesome death before like Peter did, or maybe we realize that we are like filthy rags and think God could never forgive us or use us to do anything for His kingdom. If the latter situation is where we are in our walk, we can be encouraged — God can use our humble spirit by using our tears to water the lives of others, bringing them into the Kingdom of God. If we are like Peter, God will allow us to fall so we will repent, and He can use us to create rainbows.

BATTLE PLAN: Sometimes hotshots overestimate their ability to handle challenges. It is a good thing to have confidence in ourselves and to want to do great things, but not to the point that we become cocky. A parent knows when their child has good intentions and overestimates what they can do (like Peter did). Even though our kids fail, it is encouraging to see their willingness and confidence to take on a challenge. It is an indication that they may achieve great things as an adult. I believe that God feels the same way about us. However, sometimes the training required to accomplish big things comes through suffering and tears. We must remember that Satan also sees a child of God's potential, therefore, he will do everything in his power to prevent God's will from happening. The poet Henry Sutton tells us to love sorrow and grief because it will eventually lead to rewards. Don't let the enemy convince you otherwise.

BATTLE SONG: "Tears" by Matt Hammit

SOWING TEARS, REAPING JOY

"The things that are most precious to us today have come to us through tears and pain." —J.R. Miller

There is a price to pay for everything in life. Freedom is not free—many brave men and women who fought for our freedoms understand the tremendous cost incurred to obtain it. People in the military sacrifice everything to bring blessings to others, just like Jesus did. Anyone close to them sacrifices, as well. This selflessness also applies to law enforcement officers, who give us the freedom to safely walk down our streets and sleep soundly knowing they are patrolling the area. Parents exhibit a similar sacrificial role; their children are usually their most precious gift from God. Therefore, the sleepless nights, unappreciated discipline, and devotion parents give often brings them pain and tears, as well.

Jesus understood sacrifice and knew all along that His journey was leading to the cross, yet He went willingly, so others could be free from their sins. While on this earth He said, "I have come that they may have life, and that they may have it more abundantly" (John 10:10 KJV). May we never forget the sacrifice that Jesus and others have made for us, and may we always find joy in these precious gifts that enable us to have protection, freedom, and peace.

God's word says, "Those who sow in tears shall reap in joy" (Psalm 126:5 KJV). If we are currently experiencing a season of sowing tears, we can hold onto the promise that we will someday reap joy if we keep persevering. If we are currently reaping joy, let us be a light and a beacon of hope to those who are shedding tears.

BATTLE PLAN: No matter what season we are in, it is important to remember that we cannot go back in time, we can only move forward. Thoughts of regret, unforgiveness, and hopelessness are attacks from the pit of Hell. Jesus did not say that He came to condemn us or punish us, but rather He came to give us abundant life. This means that our lives will be fuller and more bountiful. Military and police personnel fight to give us peace, safety, and freedom. The enemy wants to steal these precious gifts from us; his goal is to replace freedom with captivity, peace with anxiety, and safety with fear. God wants us to embrace the precious gift of freedom that many have fought for. He loves us so much that He gave us free will —the choice is ours to embrace the blessings that come through tears and find joy in what we have.

BATTLE SONG: "Blessings" by Laura Story

TRANSFORMING OUR MIND

"We are born crying, live complaining and die disappointed." —*Thomas Fuller*

The world teaches us to be focused on our personal goals, needs, and happiness. Whereas military culture and Christianity require us to forget about our personal agenda and concentrate on our current mission., This is hard to do and it requires rigorous training. Members of the armed forces are trained to follow lawful orders without question, work as a team, and be physically fit, so they can endure the treacherous conditions that war brings. People in the military leave everything they have and love when they are deployed— it is a total commitment, in every sense! The ability to stay mentally present in the day, and not worry about the next day or what is going on back home, is vital. Worrying takes the focus off the present and prevents people from fully engaging the task at hand. These are the same strategies that apply to a member of the Christian army, and actually, any civilian. Whether people realize it or not, they are in a spiritual battle between good against evil.

Peter said to Jesus, "We have left everything to follow you!" (Matthew 19:27 NIV). This was true, but the disciples never understood what their mission was and what "following" the Lord entailed. Peter's expectations were that of a human mindset. He was not able to see or comprehend the *big picture*. Similarly, we are often unable to understand why things happen to us. We try to use reasoning to figure things out but find ourselves frustrated, which often leads to complaining. Author Hannah Whitall Smith once said, "It all depends not on the events themselves, but how we view them. If we simply lie down, allowing them to roll over and crush us, they become an uncontrollable car of destruction. Yet if we climb into them, as riding a car of victory, they become the chariots of God to triumphantly take us onward and upward." God wants to help us rise above our hopelessness. This involves seeking His guidance and following His lead. He will be by our side as we go through the training of staying in the day and trusting Him. I often hear people who get discouraged easily say, *I'm a pessimist not an optimist; I see the cup as half empty not half full.* Someone I know adds, *That's just how I am.* My reply is usually, *so, how is that working for you?* If we refuse to change the way we think, we will never leave the past behind. Everyone is going to have a time in their life that is going to be difficult. We have the choice to lie down and be crushed or to ride to victory. We were born crying and some of us have lived complaining. However, if you are reading this you are still alive, and it is not too late to transform your mind so that you will never die disappointed about the way you chose to live.

BATTLE PLAN: "Do not be conformed to this world but be transformed by the renewing of your minds" (Romans 12:2). The world teaches: if we do everything right, life will be great, and we will be happy. That is a lie because there are things in the world that are out of our control, such as the weather. In an instant, we can lose all we love or own if a tornado or hurricane hits our area. Minister Samuel Rutherford said, "Trust God's word and His power, more than you trust your own feelings or experiences." Even though we will have hard times in life, God can get us through them. The best time for soldiers to be trained is before they go into battle, not during the fight. The same applies to us regarding spiritual battles. Training for anything in life is a commitment; a person would never enter a marathon without conditioning their body to withstand the race. The best way to reprogram our minds, is to learn the war strategies in the Bible. If we commit to the training and ask the Lord to help us, we can have victory over the battlefield of our minds.

BATTLE SONG: "By Your Side" by Tenth Avenue North

God Has a Sense of Humor

"Blessed are you who weep now, for you will laugh." —Luke 6:21 (NIV)

I had a few tough years in a row: the loss of my dad and husband, a cancer diagnosis, and financial difficulty. One summer, I was on vacation with one of my friends who was also going through a hard time in her life. We were at the beach talking about our struggles. It was really hot, so I decided to go into the ocean. I was not even in knee-deep water when a wave suddenly broke and the power of the water rushing towards me knocked me over. I got up only to encounter another wave that did the same thing. Before I attempted to get up again, I looked at my friend who was on the shore and she was laughing so hard that she had tears streaming down her face. I turned back around toward the sea and another wave broke; I decided not to stand up until the set of waves passed and the water was a little calmer. When I finally got up my bathing suit was loaded with sand and she was roaring with laughter, and so was I.

I had spent time earlier in the day trying to encourage my friend and make her smile, but I knew that her smile was forced. God, however, knew just what to do to make her laugh. I have been swimming in the ocean all my life and water that was lower than my knees never caused me to wipe out like that. I stayed in the water and got as much sand out of my suit as I could and then I made my way up the sand to my beach chair beside her. My friend preceded to tell me how funny I looked trying to stand up in such shallow water and we laughed again. That experience replaced the heaviness we felt from the weight of our problems, with a much lighter disposition. It was a perfect illustration of Proverbs 17:22 (NLT): "A cheerful heart is good medicine, but a broken spirit saps a person's strength." We felt much better after laughing and really enjoyed the rest of our day. If you are going through a season of weeping, be encouraged because God promises that you will eventually laugh. If you are experiencing a season of joy, thank God and then encourage others to brighten their day.

BATTLE PLAN: It is so important to fight the desire to stay in isolation when life is beating us down. If we make an effort to get up and engage with people, God can use them to bring a ray of hope and maybe some joy to our day. Actor Charlie Chaplin said that "A day without laughter is a day wasted." I believe he knew what he was talking about because there are so many mental and physical health benefits from laughter. Being outside in nature can also bring us joy and make us laugh; just watching animals interact with each other, or children playing can bring a smile to our faces. Visiting the beach can be therapeutic as well and even funny if you happen to see someone like me in the water. If you are not able to leave your home, invite someone over for a visit. Our walk with God is a partnership—choose today to fight the battle of despair and trust that God will hold up His end of the relationship and lift your spirits. Remember a partnership is only successful if both partners do their part.

BATTLE SONG: "Joy" by For King & Country

WAIT FOR THE PROMISE

"Sarah said, 'God has made me laugh, and all who hear will laugh with me!' She also said, 'Who would have said to Abraham that Sarah would nurse children? For I have borne him a son in his old age.'" —Genesis 21:6-7 (NKJ)

When Abraham was seventy-five years old, he was sitting near a tent door when three visitors appeared. He told his wife, Sarah, to prepare food for them. When they finished eating, the visitors prophesized to Abraham that Sarah would bear a child and Abraham would have a son. Sarah overhead the conversation and laughed because she was too old to get pregnant (Genesis 18:10-12 NIV). However, twenty-five years later when Abraham was a hundred years old and Sarah was ninety, Isaac was born.

These events tell us many things about God: His ways are not our ways (Isaiah 55:8); He keeps His promises (Joshua 21:45); and nothing is impossible for God (Luke 1:37). Are you still waiting for something that you asked God for a long time ago? If God confirmed to you that He would fulfill that promise, don't lose heart! Throughout the Bible there are numerous examples of things that would be impossible to happen in man's eyes: a talking donkey (Numbers 22:28), the parting of the red sea (Exodus 14:21), and the resurrection of Lazarus (John 11:43-45), are but a few.

With all the testimonies in the Bible of miraculous events, and God's faithfulness to honor His promises, why do we still doubt God's ability? Sarah so badly wanted a child of her own and I bet she was very depressed when her childbearing years were over and she had no children. The years of heartbreak, depression, and dreading every birthday, must have taken a toll on her. If she had only believed the promise from God, she could have had twenty-five years of peace and excitement as she anticipated the fulfillment of the prophecy. What are we currently waiting for and what are we doing while we wait?

BATTLE PLAN: "Why am I discouraged? Why is my heart so sad? I will put my hope in God! I will praise him again—my Savior and my God!" (Psalm 42:11 NLT). There is no doubt that waiting is extremely hard, but depression, fear, and anxiety only add to the dilemma; they do not speed up the process. The psalmist who wrote Psalm 42 had the right attitude; when things look hopeless it is time to dig in and continue to believe. Sometimes we must do this by encouraging ourselves. God's word is either true or false—it cannot be both. Therefore, while we wait for the promise, we need to live life to the fullest and leave our cares at the foot of the cross.

BATTLE SONG: "While I'm Waiting" by John Waller

THE LAUGHTER OF GOD

"The wicked plot against the godly; they snarl at them in defiance, but the Lord just laughs for he sees their day of judgement coming." —Psalm 37:12-13 (NLT)

Pilots while flying over terrain can see for miles what is happening on the ground below them. Where their visibility is limited, God's is not. He is capable of seeing everything that is going on. Sometimes God tells us to go to a foreign land and we are anxious of what lies on the path ahead of us. Even though God told us to take this route, it doesn't mean that we are not going to encounter landmines. As much as we plan and think we are prepared for every scenario, there always seems to be an element of surprise from the enemy of our soul. Our reaction to his attacks is usually, *"How did this happen? Where is God?"*

When I was leaving Uganda in 2014, I thought I did a good job planning my departure, however, when my driver picked me up to take me to the Entebbe Airport at 11:00 p.m. to catch my 1:10 a.m. flight, my thoughts were: *"What was I thinking when I booked this flight?!"* I had no idea how to navigate the airport or if there would be many people there that late at night. However, I had no choice, but to trust God and stick to the plan.

The airport was easy to navigate, but there were hardly any people there. When I got to customs there was a small line of people, mostly white men. When I got to the customs officer, I gave him my passport, visa, and airline ticket. After he looked at everything, he told me that he could not let me through customs because my visa wasn't stamped with my arrival date. He preceded to tell me that I had to go to the US Embassy, and they would tell me what to do. I never expected this to happen! I said to the customs officer, "The embassy isn't open, and I have no way of getting there, even if it was." His reply was, "There is nothing I can do, and you need to get out of line." When I heard that, I said to myself, *Jesus help!!* My Italian boldness kicked in and I told him: "It is not my fault the customs officer didn't stamp my passport when I arrived in Uganda, and I am NOT getting out of this line!" Once again, he told me to get out the line because I was holding it up. I turned around and there was a long line behind me. All of a sudden, I remembered that I had my ticket to Uganda with my luggage tags in my carry-on bag and I took them out and showed the officer. He told me that it still didn't change the fact that my visa wasn't stamped upon arrival. Suddenly, a man that worked at the airport approached us and asked what the problem was. I explained and showed him my ticket to Uganda, my luggage tags, and my visa. He told the customs officer to let me through and I made my way to my gate.

Once I got to the gate and sat down, emotions of fear crept in, and I couldn't wait to board the plane. When I was fighting to get through customs, I wasn't fearful, I was bold and determined. However, when I finally sat in a seat at the gate, everything hit me. This situation gave me a small idea of what soldiers on the battlefield might experience; while fighting they are not fearful, but determined to defeat their enemy, but when they are back at their base and reflect on what transpired their emotions surface. Once I boarded the plane to London, I thought about the events—everything changed when I prayed, *Jesus help!* When we find ourselves blindsided, all we have to do is cry out to the Lord and ask for His help.

BATTLE PLAN: God always helped me when I was in trouble in Uganda. When we follow God's orders, His plans don't fail. God knows the beginning from the end and every move Satan is going to make, and He laughs at the enemy's attempts. Just like someone in the armed forces needs to take and follow orders to win a battle, so do we to win the war against despair!

BATTLE SONG: "Say the Name" by Joni Lamb

THE JOY THAT COMES FROM HOPE

"Hope fills the afflicted soul with such inward joy and consolation, that it can laugh while tears are in the eye, sigh and sing all in a breath; it is called 'The rejoicing of hope'" —William Gurnall

Life is full of surprises —some are good, and some are bad. However, some things are not always what they appear to be. When I met with my ovarian oncologist, he ordered a scan to make sure that my cancer hadn't spread. The results showed that I would have to deal with thyroid cancer after I healed from my ovary surgery. Six months later, I had the left lobe of my thyroid out and I was home recovering and waiting for the pathology results. The morning the doctor called me with the results, God had led me to the story of Esau and Jacob in the Old Testament (Genesis 25:27-34 NLT). These two men were brothers. Esau was a great hunter and Jacob was not, but Jacob knew how to cook. One day, Esau came back from the wilderness exhausted and very hungry. He approached his brother and asked for a bowl of stew. Jacob said that he could have some stew, but only if he would give up his birthright as the eldest son: being the patriarch of the family and receiving the inheritance when their father died. "Look I'm dying of starvation!" said Esau. "What good is my birthright to me now?" (Genesis 25:32 NLT). Esau agreed to Jacob's request, but once his stomach was full, he had big regrets. Although his hunger had him in a weakened state, he wasn't close to death. My takeaway from my morning reading was that things are not always what they appeared to be, and I went about my day.

My doctor called me in the afternoon with my pathology results. He told me that I did have cancer in my thyroid and that one lymph node was not cancer. Since he only took out one of my thyroid lobes, I had to have another surgery to remove the other lobe. He made an appointment for me to see him the following week and we hung up. Shortly after I thought...*what did he mean that "one" of the lymph nodes wasn't cancer; were the other nodes cancer?* Almost immediately after I had that thought, God reminded me of my reading that morning that things are not always what they appear to be. I decided to trust God and not think or worry about it. When I met with my doctor the next week, I asked him why he said that "one of my lymph nodes was not cancer." His reply was, "Oh, because I only took one lymph node out." I laughed and silently thanked God for leading me to the story of Jacob and Esau. When we find ourselves uncertain of our future, how do proceed? Who do we turn to for advice and comfort? When we spend time with our heavenly Father, He can give us words of hope that will allow us to be optimistic rather than fearful while we wait to see what our future will bring.

BATTLE PLAN: I shared my story because it is so important for us to spend time daily praying for guidance and reading God's word. Because I spent time in the morning reading my Bible and devotionals and believing what God showed me, I was able to have peace the whole week before my doctor's appointment. If I chose not to read, or to read but not believe what God was showing me, I would have worried about cancer being in my lymph nodes the whole week. Once we open the door to worry, Satan has access to attack. He will launch darts of doubt, fear, and discouragement. Then, when we get the news that things are better than we thought, the enemy takes a victory lap because he not only made us miserable, but he kept us from being productive. We must not give Satan the satisfaction. When the devil fires thoughts of doubt, throw them out immediately!

BATTLE SONG: "Take You At Your Word" by Cody Carnes, featuring Benjamin William Hastings

A TIME TO MOURN, AND A TIME TO DANCE

—ECCLESIASTES 3:4

GOD'S FAITHFULNESS

"When the sun finally drops below the horizon in the early evening, evidence of its work remains for some time. The skies continue to glow for a full hour after its departure. In the same way, when a good or a great person's life comes to its final sunset, the skies of this world are illuminated until long after he is out of view. Such a person does not die from this world, for when he departs, he still speaks." — *Henry Ward Beecher*

My dad had been sick for a while with heart and kidney disease. He was going from hospital to rehab and rehab to hospital; it was a vicious cycle. His only wish was to be home in his own house. One day I was on my way to work when I got a call from the rehab nurse saying that an ambulance was taking my dad to the hospital again. Luckily, I wasn't too far from the exit off the highway to the hospital. The bottom line was that my dad needed surgery and he refused to have it. To stay alive, he would have to do dialysis and he said no to that. as well. We planned to take him home in the morning. My brother Joe and I slept on the chairs in my dad's hospital room that night.

During the night, my dad slipped into a coma. We still took him home in the morning. My daughter was extremely close to my father and wanted to be holding his hand when he died, so she stayed at his house with me. I was by mom's side when she died, and I also wanted to be by my dad's side when he passed away.

My father had been home for two days and his breathing was very shallow; the hospice nurse said that he could die at any time. I called my daughter to let her know what was happening. She was working an hour away from his house and would be driving home in rush-hour traffic; we prayed that she would make it to his house before he died. My dad's breathing began to return to normal by the time she arrived. My daughter and I had a nightly routine: we would watch TV until 11:00 p.m. and then I would take a nap because I had to give my dad his medicine at 3:00 a.m. He was in a hospital bed in his living room, and I would lay on the couch next to the bed while my daughter watched a movie in the recliner. The next night while I was napping, the movie my daughter was watching ended and she decided to swab my dad's mouth with some water. She went over to the bed and saw that his breaths were far apart; she picked up his hand and yelled, "Mom get up!" I jumped up and I stood next to him as he was breathing his last breath. We both started to cry, but at the same time we said, "Absent from the body, present with the Lord" (2 Corinthians 5:8), and we smiled as the tears streamed down our faces.

God was so faithful to grant both our wishes. My daughter was holding his hand and I was by his side. God gave us the desires of our hearts during this difficult time so that we would know that He was with us; it was so comforting. The night I dreaded coming had arrived and I had a myriad of feelings: sadness and joy at the same time. I guess I can best describe it as a sun-shower. I don't know if you have ever experienced a time when it was raining, but the sun was still shining. We were raining tears when my dad took his last breath, however, the "Son" was shining. The minute my dad left our sides, he was in the presence of Jesus.

My daughter shared this story of God's faithfulness at my father's funeral. Some people came up to her afterward and told her that they were no longer afraid of dying. After the funeral, my siblings and our kids went back to my dad's house. While we were there, a rain shower was going on outside. When I left his house to go home, the rain had stopped and there was a rainbow in the sky across the street. In the book of Genesis, it states that God put a rainbow in the sky after Noah's flood. This was a covenant (promise) that He would never destroy the earth again by a flood. I believe God allowed me to see the rainbow, as a reminder that His promise of eternal life is true, and my dad was with Him in Heaven. If you are mourning the death of a loved one, know that the Lord is with you, and He can bring healing in this difficult season of your life.

BATTLE PLAN: Even though I never doubted God's promise of salvation, the sky was illuminated with a kaleidoscope of colors that showed me that God was with me, and my dad was with Him. Clergyman Henry Ward Beecher's quote also came true for me; sometimes when I am perplexed, the advice my dad gave me when I was growing up pops in my head— he *is* still speaking. to me. I pray that this story brings you comfort if you are facing death, or you are losing a loved one. God's word says, "Blessed are those who mourn, for they shall be comforted (Matthew 5:4 NIV). Cry out to the Lord and He will comfort you.

BATTLE SONG: "Cry Out to Jesus" by Third Day

MOURNING BUT STILL MOVING

"So the victory that day was turned into mourning for all the people." —*2 Samuel 19:2 (NKJ)*

The scripture above is in reference to King David's loss of his son Absalom. Prior to this event, Absalom became popular with many people in David's kingdom and eventually, there were more people who wanted Absalom to be king than there were who wanted David as king. There were no elections in those days, so David would remain king until he died. However, Absalom took the throne by force, causing David and his men to flee for their lives, and the battle for control continued. One day, Absalom was riding a mule "under the thick boughs of a great terebinth tree, and his head got caught in the terebinth, so he was left hanging between heaven and earth. And the mule under him went on. Now a certain man saw it and told Joab" (David's commander) and Joab said, "You just saw him! And why did you not strike him to the ground'" (2 Samuel 18:9-11 NKJ)? Then, Joab went where Absalom was and killed him.

When King David found out about his son's death he cried. Instead of Joab sympathizing with David he said, "Today you have disgraced all your servants who today have saved your life, the lives of your sons and daughters...in that you love your enemies and hate your friends...for today I perceive that if Absalom had lived and all of us had died today then it would have pleased you. Now therefore, arise, go out and speak comfort to your servants. For I swear by the Lord, if you do not go out, not one will stay with you this night" (2 Samuel 19:5-7 NKJ). Victory usually comes at a high price and God truly understands the pain that it can bring.

The takeaway from this story is that it is okay to weep over the loss of a loved one, but not to the point that we are no longer engaged in the world around us. We still have work to do while we are on this earth. When Moses died, God told Joshua, "Arise, go over this Jordan, you and all this people, to the land which I am giving to them—the children of Israel" (Joshua 1:2 NKJ). The battle between good and evil in the world is not going to end until Jesus Christ comes back. Therefore, we must keep going even when our heart is breaking and

112

our desire to continue is gone. The Lord told Joshua, "Be strong and of good courage; do not be afraid, nor dismayed, for the Lord your God is with you wherever you go" (Joshua 1:9 NKJ). This promise is true for us, too! If God calls us to do something, He will be with us and help us accomplish the task, as long as we are obedient to His guidance.

BATTLE PLAN: The enemy loves to divide us, so that he can easily conquer us. God's word says, "If a kingdom be divided against itself, that kingdom cannot stand" (Mark 3:24 KJV). We often think of people when we hear this verse, but what about our spirit or our relationship with God? Will our loyalty to Him waver when we lose someone we love? Mourning is a part of life—even Jesus wept when Lazarus died (John 11:35). However, there comes a time when we arise from our sorrow. David and Joshua, like Jesus, arose from their sadness and kept going because they had a mission to accomplish, and so do we!

BATTLE SONG: "The Hurt & The Healer" by MercyMe

THE BURDENS WE CARRY

"Rejoice with those who rejoice; mourn with those who mourn." —Romans 12:15 (NIV)

Being self-sufficient can be a good thing, but it can also be a bad thing when we refuse to accept help when we need it. God did not intend for us to walk through life alone, especially when we are struggling with injuries, disease, or financial issues. Sometimes God allows our burdens to be heavy, so we will cry out to Him. Other times, He may send someone to help us.

When Jesus was badly beaten and forced to carry His cross to the place where He would be crucified, many people along the path were crying. I believe that God allowed Simon to help Jesus carry His cross to be an example for us. "As they led Jesus away, a man named Simon, who was from Cyrene happened to be coming in from the countryside. The soldiers seized him and put the cross on him and made him carry it behind Jesus" (Luke 23:26). There is no mention anywhere in the Bible that Jesus said, *I got this; I don't need your help.* That is because He never said that, and He allowed Simon to help carry the burden of His cross.

When God made Adam, He took one of his ribs and created Eve from it (Genesis 2:21-22 NIV). God knew what life would be like for us and that we would need support and help from others to survive. Unfortunately, our society has become one that elevates people who are totally independent. However, the truth is that when we claim that we don't need anyone, we are acting prideful. "God resists the proud but gives grace to the humble. Therefore, humble yourselves under the mighty hand of God, that He may exalt you in due time, casting all your care upon Him, for He cares for you" (1 Peter 5:5-7 NKJ). Pride is one of Satan's characteristics, not a trait of Jesus who depended on God to guide Him. If Jesus had to depend on God, how much more do we need to depend on Him?

BATTLE PLAN: When Jesus resurrected from the grave, those who were crying at the crucifixion were now rejoicing with Him. We can rejoice too because Jesus will always be with us, helping us carry our burdens (Matthew 11:29-30 NIV). What burdens are you currently carrying alone: depression, sickness, maybe loneliness? Why not lay them upon the Lord's shoulders? God's plans for our future are good, not bad (Jeremiah 29:11 NIV). Therefore, we should not fear what is ahead of us, because we never have to face the difficult seasons of life alone.

BATTLE SONG: "Shoulders" by For King & Country

DO WE DANCE OR POUT?

"Meanwhile the older son was in the fields working. When he returned home, he heard music and dancing in the house"—Luke 15:25 (NLT)

When military personnel or children who are away at college return home, the family celebrates their return. The opening scripture is part of a story that Jesus told the people. This parable is about a man's youngest son who asked his father for his inheritance early. Once the son got his inheritance, he traveled throughout the land partying and enjoying life—until he found himself penniless and starving. He then decided to go home, ask his father's forgiveness, and then ask his dad for a job. When the son returned the father was so excited that he had a big feast for him with music and dancing.

The man's older son in the parable worked hard for his father and never asked him for anything. When he arrived home and witnessed the celebration going on for his brother, he was angry. His dad had never thrown a party for him, even though he was the son that remained loyal and worked hard. The father begged the older son to come in and join in the celebration, but he said no and explained how he felt about his brother's return. His dad responded, "dear son, you have always stayed by me and everything I have is yours. We had to celebrate this happy day. For your brother was dead and has come back to life! He was lost, but now he is found" (Luke 15:31 NLT). The father's love for his boys was unconditional; it wasn't based on their behavior. It doesn't mean that the dad was happy with the younger son's behavior, but the dad had forgiven him.

The older son was resentful and chose to pout, but that did not stop the celebration for his brother. Everyone was enjoying themselves while the older son was miserable. We have all had times when we have been overlooked for our good deeds and others have been rewarded for bad deeds. However, God tells us to "rejoice with those who rejoice; mourn with those who mourn" (Romans 12:15 NIV). If we do this, we prevent Satan from winning the division battle.

BATTLE PLAN: The world tells us to work hard, be committed to our job, and we will be rewarded. However, sometimes people are not appreciated and passed over for a promotion. God says the same thing about us being rewarded for our faithfulness, hard work, and loyalty, but sometimes our rewards are not given to us while on Earth, but rather in Heaven. Satan wants to divide and conquer families, countries, and any relationship that provides us love and support. Although his warfare is very strategic, it can only be successful if we cooperate with his devious plan. In John 21:18-19 Jesus tells the apostle Peter how he will die, and it is gruesome. Peter looked at the apostle John and asked Jesus, "What about this man?" (John 21:21 NKJ). Jesus said to Peter, "If I will that he remains till I come, what is that to you? You follow me" (verse 22). In other words, the Lord is telling us not to compare ourselves with others; He knows that once we start doing this it opens the door for Satan to tempt us to be jealous, resentful, or mad at God. You see, God had a plan for Peter to be the head of his church and for John to write about what Heaven will be like (which is the book of Revelation). God wanted them to be focused on their mission. Just like people in the military have a specific job to perform on their team, we have a specific part to play here on Earth. We should be focused on that and not what everyone else is doing. When our mission on Earth is over, God will call us home and there will be rewards and dancing. So, let's focus on our mission and rejoice with those who come home.

BATTLE SONG: "Fix My Eyes" by For King & Country

WHEN WE MUST MOVE

"And Lot lifted his eyes and saw all the plain of the Jordan, that it was well watered everywhere (before the Lord destroyed Sodom and Gomorrah) like the garden of the Lord... Then Lot chose for himself all the plain of the Jordan." — Genesis 13:10-11 (NKJ)

Sometimes things look great, but they can be the worst thing for us. So, it was for Lot when he chose to live near Sodom. In Genesis 11, we read that Abram and his wife, Sarai, lived with his father and his nephew Lot. However, God instructed Abram to take his family and leave his father's house and go "to a land that I will show you. I will make a great nation; and you shall be a blessing" (Genesis 12:1-2 NKJ). Even though God did not tell Abram where his final destination was, he left his homeland and started on the journey. His nephew Lot, left with his family as well and traveled with Abram. They ended up settling in Egypt, but they were forced to leave there (Genesis 12:14-20). While traveling to a new place they realized that the land lacked resources to support their livestock, so they knew they had to separate. Abram gave Lot the choice of going to the east or to the west. Lot saw that the land of Jordan looked better, so he traveled east.

When I read the story of Abram and Lot, I might have taken the land to the east as well. I am a planner, and after evaluating the needs of my animals and what the land offered, it would have been the most logical choice to make. However, Abram wasn't thinking about his needs because he gave Lot the opportunity to choose what he wanted, and Abram would go in the other direction. This act of selflessness shows two things: Abram trusted God and he loved Lot. Although the land to the east looked the best, Abram ended up in a better place. In fact, Lot lost everything, even his wife, when God destroyed Sodom and Gomorrah (Genesis 19:26).

Sodom and Gomorrah were filled with evil people, yet Lot still stayed on the outskirts of Sodom knowing how bad the culture was. Nevertheless, God saved him and his daughters from destruction because Abram asked God to. Lot's wife would have been saved as well if she hadn't looked back (Genesis 19). When the angels came to destroy Sodom and save Lot, they told Lot that he had to move quickly, or he would be destroyed with the city.

Lot made it safely to the town of Zoar. When Abram and Lot separated, God told Abram to look around and all the land that he could see was his (Genesis 13:14). The takeaway from this story is that God took care of both Abram and Lot, but their outcomes were very different. Abram was safe where he was, and Lot needed rescuing. What role in this story is closest to our current situation? Have we made a bad choice because it wasn't what it appeared to be? Is God asking us to move on to a better place, but we refuse to go? Perhaps, we have stepped out into the unknown and we are uncertain of our future. Either way, if we trust God and follow His guidance, He can bring us to better days!

BATTLE PLAN: Both Abram and Lot moved when God told them to, and they never gave up persevering. However, Lot focused on himself, and Abram trusted God. When God gives us the choice to go to the east or the west, what factors do we consider? Lot looked at what the land had to offer, whereas Abram left the decision up to God by giving Lot first choice. The enemy will try to persuade us to go in the wrong direction. Remember—God will never contradict Himself (His guidance will line up with the Bible) and Satan always twists scripture a little to trick us.

BATTLE SONG: "Move" by MercyMe

DANCING IN THE FIRE

"Let them praise his name with dancing." —*Psalm 149:3 (NIV)*

Although some of us may feel that today's society puts pressure on us to conform to what it believes, this has been happening throughout the ages. King Nebuchadnezzar of Babylon reigned in 582 BC. During that time, the Babylonians raided the tribe of Judah and many of the Jewish people were taken captive. The king made a gold image and demanded that the people in the kingdom worship it. Whoever refused to worship the idol would be thrown into a blazing furnace (Daniel 3:1-7 NIV). There were three Jewish boys named Shadrach, Meshack, and Abednego, who refused to worship the idol; they said that their God would rescue them from the fire, but even if He didn't, they would rather die than worship a false god (Daniel 3:16-18 NIV).

King Nebuchadnezzar was enraged, and he gave the boys one more chance to worship the gold image. When they refused, they were thrown into the blazing furnace. While the king and his soldiers were looking at the boys walking in the flames, they noticed another person in the fire. The king couldn't believe that the boys were not instantly burned to death and said, "the form of the fourth is like the Son of God" (Daniels 3:25 NKJ). When Nebuchadnezzar let the boys out of the furnace, they did not even smell of smoke. The king elevated the boy's status and told the Babylonian people that if anyone talked badly about their God, they "will be cut into pieces" (Daniel 3:21-30 NIV). This story is not only written in the Old Testament of the Bible, but it is also written in the Jewish Canon. In 2015, ancient tablets were discovered in Iraq and there was information written on them about the Jews captivity in Babylon. Archeologists said that the writings proved that the Jews were in captivity. The three Jewish boys put their faith and trust in God, and He came through for them. What or who do we put our faith in when depression, addiction, or illness is holding us captive? Do we try to fight this enemy on our own? If so, how is that working out?

BATTLE PLAN: God allowed the Jews to be captured by the Babylonians because most of them had turned away from Him and He wanted them to turn back to Him. However, Shadrach, Meshack, and Abednego still honored God and His ways. Therefore, God not only saved the boys from the fire, but He also put it on the king's heart to elevate their status in the kingdom. I imagine the boys where praising God and maybe even dancing. When we put our faith and trust in the God who created the universe, He can not only free us from captivity, but also use our lives to show the world who He is—our heavenly Father who loves us and will always be with us, even when we must go through the fire. The enemy of our soul will have people threaten to destroy us, but we must not fall for this trap! Remember, Satan was an angel, created by God, who was thrown out of Heaven; therefore, God is much more powerful than he is.

BATTLE SONG: "Dancing Through the Fire" by Jordan Feliz

I'LL BE HOME FOR CHRISTMAS

"You have turned for me my mourning into joyful dancing." — Psalm 30:11 *(NLT)*

The holidays are a time when families gather together and celebrate. In the 1940s Bing Crosby recorded the popular song, "I'll Be Home for Christmas." The song made some people sad because they had family members fighting in World War II. However, it actually brought hope to many of the soldiers fighting overseas. Today, many people dread the holidays because it is a reminder that the people they love are no longer with them.

Christmas was always my favorite holiday; however, the year my dad and husband died, I was not looking forward to it. My mom had died three years prior, and I was missing all of them. I decided I would put up my Christmas tree, so I opened the box of ornaments to start decorating it. I always had a special place in front of the tree to put my grandparent's ornaments, and I decided I would hang my parent's angel ornaments and my husband's icicle ornaments there as well. As I was hanging them, I began to cry—actually sob is a better word. Suddenly, a thought came to my mind, which was more like a voice in my head that said, *"rejoice and be glad, they are all with me in Heaven and will celebrate Jesus' birth with Him."* I instantly smiled when I thought… *"they are all pain free and with the Lord."* I not only finished decorating the tree, but I sang Christmas carols while doing it! That day I moved on to another season of my life—one that took away the sorrow and fear of being alone and brought me peace and joy. If you are in a season of life that is filled with solitude and sorrow, seek God for encouragement. He is close to the brokenhearted (Psalm 34:18 NLT) and wants to bring you healing and joy. However, you must choose to let go of the sorrow of winter, so God can bring you the joy of spring.

BATTLE PLAN: If the enemy of your soul can keep you focused on what you lost and not what you have, he will be able to steal your joy and keep you in a saddened state. During World War II, the thoughts of Christmas for people who had loved ones fighting abroad was a time of sorrow. However, it was that same song that gave some of the warriors fighting in the war—hope. Since our eternal home is in Heaven, Earth is like a foreign land in which we are caught in a battle between good and evil. Therefore, we must have hope and keep on fighting the attacks coming against us. Writer J. R. Miller said, "Christ is building His Kingdom with the broken things of the earth. People desire only the strong, successful, victorious, and unbroken things in life to build their kingdoms…He [Christ] can take a life crushed by pain or sorrow and make it a harp whose music will be total praise." When we choose to dodge the bullets of depression and the captivity of sorrow, God can strengthen us, so we can defeat the enemy. Colossians 3:2 (NIV) says, "Set your minds on things above, not on earthly things." I really understand the meaning of that scripture now. Life on Earth is so short and eternity is forever, it won't be too long before we see our family members who are in Heaven. In the meantime, we need to be grateful and enjoy the blessings we have, while fulfilling the call that God has on our lives.

BATTLE SONG: "Graves Into Gardens" by Elevation Worship

RESTORATION & DANCING

"The art of living is more like wrestling than dancing." —Marcus Aurelius

Throughout the ages, people have wrestled with doing the right thing and satisfying their fleshly desires. It began with Eve in the garden of Eden when she ate the forbidden fruit. If, however, the serpent (Satan) had not tempted her by twisting God's words, would Eve have sinned? Afterall, she had never even imagined disobeying God before and was perfectly happy with all the other food in the garden. This act of disobedience led her husband astray as well. I guess there is some truth to the saying: *"One bad apple spoils the whole bunch."*

The Jewish people in the Old Testament of the Bible struggled with sin and idolatry on many occasions. The kings became self-righteous and some of them worshipped false gods, which caused the people to stray from God, as well. Prophets were sent to warn the people to turn back to God, and if they didn't, He would pour out His wrath on them. When the people ignored the warning of the prophets, God allowed them to be taken captive by their enemies.

Some may think that is harsh treatment; however, earthly parents discipline their children because they love them and want to protect them from evil. Good parents don't allow their children to continue being disobedient. Similarly, it is God's love for us that causes Him to discipline us.

Even though God's people were taken into captivity, He never gave up on them. All the people had to do was repent and turn back to Him and His ways, and He would bless them. Jeremiah 31:3-4 (NLT) puts it this way, "Long ago the Lord said to Israel: I have loved you, my people, with an everlasting love, with unfailing love I have drawn you to myself. I will rebuild you my virgin Israel. You will again be happy and dance merrily with your tambourines." God wants to bless His children, just like we want to bless our kids. If we are in a season of captivity rather than blessing, we need to reflect on how we got there. Are we worshipping false gods: money, sex, power, etc.? If so, we can be encouraged because God is still there waiting for us to

124

repent and turn back to Him. Once we do, He can turn our despairing hearts into one of dancing.

BATTLE PLAN: When Jesus was in the garden of Gethsemane, He said to Peter, "Watch and pray, so that you will not fall into temptation. The spirit is willing, but the flesh is weak" (Matthew 26:41 NIV). Instead of Peter watching out for temptation, he fell asleep. When the soldiers came and captured Jesus, the disciples went into hiding. Jesus not only forgave Peter for denying he knew Him, but He built Peter up and elevated him in the kingdom. We must not let the enemy trick us into believing that God will not forgive us for our sins. "The plans of the Lord stand firm forever; the purposes of his heart through all generations" (Psalm 33:11 NIV). God's promise of forgiveness is for anyone who believes in Him and His Son's gift of salvation. When we trade our sorrows for the joy of the Lord, we can dance merrily like the people of Israel.

BATTLE SONG: "I'm Trading My Sorrows" by Darrell Evans

SINGING & DANCING IN THE RAIN

"The person who dances with you in the rain will most likely walk with you in the storm."—Unknown

As a child, I loved watching the movie *Singing in the Rain*. It starred Debbie Reynolds and Gene Kelly. There is one scene in the movie where Gene Kelly is walking down the street with an umbrella in the pouring rain. He begins singing and dancing on the sidewalk and in the street, which was extremely impressive. At one point he starts jumping and splashing in the puddles like a child. He had no idea that a police officer was watching him and looking at him like he was either crazy or drunk. I occasionally google that scene from the movie on YouTube and it always brings a smile to my face to see someone so carefree. I believe that it makes God smile when He sees us singing and dancing during the rainstorms of our lives.

It is easy for us to be optimistic and happy when the sun is shining and things are going well; we believe that God is with us, and He loves us. However, most of us struggle when the flood waters are rising and we cannot control the situation. We start thinking…*where is God and how can He allow this?* The enemy wants to confuse us into thinking that if we are good, things will always go well. However, that theory is not true because Jesus said this about God, "He causes his sun to rise on the evil and the good and sends rain on the righteous and the unrighteous" (Matthew 5:45 NIV). Sometimes God lifts the protection He has around us and allows the enemy to have his way with us to test us, like He did with Job (Job 1 NIV), or to get us to turn back to Him if we have become a prodigal child (Luke 15 NIV). God wants what is best for us. Although Job lost everything and suffered, God not only restored everything to him, but He gave "Job twice as much as he had before" (Job 42:10 NIV). It is through trusting and persevering that we can have victory.

God told His people in the past, "Fear not, for I have redeemed you; I have called you by your name, you are Mine. When you pass through the waters, I will be with you; and through the rivers, they shall not overflow you." (Isaiah 43:1-2 NKJ). His promises never expire, so we know that He will be with us too. How do we face the rainstorms in our lives—do we embrace them and dance in the puddles, or do we retreat and complain? There will be storms in our lives and some of them will be severe, however, we can be encouraged because God will be the one who is going to dance with us in rain and walk with us during the storms of our lives.

BATTLE PLAN: The enemy will never give up trying to destroy us. The apostle Peter's name was Simon before Jesus changed it. "The Lord said, 'Simon, Simon! Indeed, Satan has asked for you, that he may sift you as wheat. But I have prayed for you, that your faith should not fail; and when you have returned to Me, strengthen your brethren'" (Luke 22:31-33). Simon did fail, he denied knowing Christ three times. However, he needed to fail, so that he could see that he wasn't as great as he thought he was and that he could do nothing apart from the Lord. Sometimes we need to learn this lesson too, and it's encouraging to know that Jesus prays for us. As much as we try not to, we are going to fail during our life (Matthew 26:41 NKJ). When we do, we need to ask God to forgive us and give us the strength to go on. Each time we continue on our journey, our faith and trust in God increases. Perhaps someday, we will be filled with God's inexpressible joy, and we will find ourselves dancing and singing during the severest storms of our life!

BATTLE SONG: "Happy Dance" by MercyMe

A TIME TO CAST AWAY STONES, AND A TIME TO GATHER STONES—ECCLESIASTES 3:5A

Perfect Love Casts Out Fear

"There is no fear in love, but perfect love casts out fear, because fear involves torment. But he who fears has not been made perfect in love." —1 John 4:18 (NKJ)

I t is amazing how people find unimaginable strength when someone they love is in danger. There are stories of moms lifting cars off of their children and husbands physically covering their families from flying debris as a tornado rips through their neighborhood. Sometimes complete strangers commit the same brave acts because they value all life and instinctively protect others. If humans can "cast away their fear" to help others, why can't they believe that God would do the same for them? He loves us so much that He sent His only Son to die for us.

The opening scripture states that "he who fears has not been made perfect in love." If we have allowed God into our lives and hearts, then His love is inside us; as we absorb it, we begin to have compassion, devotion, and respect for others. When we have those feelings for the people we don't know, we know that it is God's unconditional love pouring out of us. We begin to understand how God can love us even though we are sinners. Once we can comprehend the depth of His love, we do not need to fear anything because we realize that He will work everything that happens to us for our good, because we love Him (Roman 8:28 NLT) and He loves us. When we encounter fear and anxiety, we simply need to cast it out and ask God to help us. When we resist the devil, the author of fear, he will flee (James 4:7 NLT). Theologian Martin Luther said, "all the cunning of the devil is exercised in trying to tear us away from the word." Therefore, be prepared for the battle, don't wait until you are being attacked to look for promises in the Bible from God. Being unprepared is like a soldier waiting until the enemy is upon him before he starts to look for his gun. A good warrior always carries his weapon and never underestimates his enemy.

BATTLE STATEGY: Know God's word! According to Genesis 3, ever since God created human beings, Satan has been at work trying to convince them that God doesn't love them, and He does not have their best interest at heart. The devil's first victim was Eve, when she was in the garden of Eden. Although she knew not to eat from the tree in the middle of the garden, the enemy convinced her to eat of the fruits by telling her that the fruit from the tree would make her wise. She not only ate from the tree but convinced Adam, her husband, to eat from it also. Adam and Eve could have eaten from all the other trees in the garden, but the enemy convinced them that they needed to have that fruit as well. His tactics never change, when we are satisfied with what we have, he will dangle things in front of us that God forbids: sexual immorality, our neighbors' possessions, etc. If he can get us to contemplate it, we have let him in the door. "Be careful who you trust, the devil was once an angel" (author unknown). The best defense against Satan is knowing God's promises and commandments. Always have your sword with you, which is God's word, because you never know when you will encounter the enemy.

BATTLE SONG: "Perfect Love" by Jeremy Camp

Don't Cast Away Your Confidence

"Do not cast away your confidence, which has great reward. For you have need of endurance, so that after you have done the will of God, you may receive the promise."
—Hebrews 10:35-36

Sometimes we grow weary while waiting for God to answer our prayers. The apostle Peter said that God's timetable is not the same as ours — "with the Lord a day is like a thousand years and a thousand years are like a day" (2 Peter 3:8 NIV). We are so used to having instant gratification, fast food, and Siri to immediately answer our questions that we grow impatient very easily. When we put our confidence in the knowledge and things of the world, we do not know how to handle a situation when nobody has the answer to our dilemma. The apostle Peter tells us that we do not have answers because sometimes God doesn't want us too. If everything came easy in life, how would we build up strength or trust in God? People in the military go through extensive training, so that they will be confident in their ability to handle any situation. God puts us through a training as well, so that we can build faith in Him.

When I think of endurance, I sometimes think of a Rocky movie. He was a boxer who could take a lot of punches. In one movie he was down on the ground and his opponent started walking away because he thought he had won the fight. Suddenly, he hears Rocky saying that he didn't hear any bell ring. Rocky gets up and wins the fight. He endured the pain and received the promise of victory. When the apostle Peter told the people that they needed to endure, he also told them that "we are more than conquerors through Him who loved us' (Romans 8:37 NIV). Our confidence should not only be in ourselves, but also in God. When we put our faith and trust in Him, He gives us the desire to get up when we are knocked down, so that we can endure that last round and achieve victory.

Throughout the ages God gave His people the strength to persevere, and He always will. When we find ourselves doubting His faithfulness, all we have to do is read Hebrews 11 to be reminded of it. The very first verse in that chapter says, "Faith is the substance of things hoped for, the evidence of things not seen." This tells us that when it appears that God is not working in our situation, He is; the *"seeing is believing theory"* is not always true when it comes to Christianity. If we continue reading Hebrews 11, we will see all the times that God came through for His people. Remember, He created the universe from nothing, there were no architect plans, building codes, or building supplies. He *spoke* everything in the universe into existence. Everything is possible with God!

BATTLE PLAN: Whatever season you find yourself in today, remember that when you put your confidence in God's ability and not your own, you will receive the promise. Therefore, *"Do not cast away your confidence"* in God, but rather cast out your doubt, fear, and worry. Throwing off all that hinders will not only strengthen you, but it will help you endure the season. When the next season begins your faith will be even stronger!

BATTLE SONG: "Cheering You On" by For King & Country

CAST AWAY THE STONE OF WORRY

"Cast all your anxiety on him, because he cares for you." —*1 Peter 5:7 (NIV)*

We all make mistakes, and sometimes reap the repercussions of those bad choices. However, if we add up the good things we have done and the bad things we did, most of us would see that the good outweighed the bad. Why then, do we focus on the negative rather than the positive? One of the reasons is that today's society is full of judgmental people who are so quick to point out our mistakes; even worse than that is the fact that many of them will not even accept a sincere apology. As such, how do you live with this condemnation?

Jesus had a way of dealing with those who didn't live up to the standards that they set for others. One day the Pharisees brought a woman to Him, who was caught committing adultery. They asked Jesus what they should do with her. The law back then required that a person be stoned to death if they were caught in this act. Once again, the religious leaders were trying to catch the Messiah in a trap, so they would have evidence against Him. Have you noticed that some human beings today still try this type of manipulation? Jesus' reaction was not at all what they expected: He began to write on the ground and told the accusers that those who were without sin to cast the first stone, and He continued writing in the dirt with his finger. The Bible does not mention what Jesus was writing, but some think He may have been listing the sins of the men accusing the woman. One by one the accusers dropped their stones and walked away. Jesus told the woman that He was not going to condemn her either (John 8:1-11 NLT).

I love this story because it sets us free from worrying about what others think about us, or what they may accuse us of. We only have to worry about what God thinks of us and if we have sinned, we need to repent and ask for forgiveness. Romans 8:1 (NIV) says that "There is, therefore, no condemnation for those who are in Christ Jesus." Once we confess our sins and repent, we are covered by the blood of Christ. Henry Ward Beecher said, "The strength of a man consists in finding out the way in which God is going and going that way too." The woman caught in the act of adultery was Mary

Magdalene who became one of Jesus' biggest followers. She truly understood the concept of grace (mercy when you don't deserve it). She went the way the Lord was going and by following Christ, she grew strong. After Jesus' crucifixion, she went to His tomb looking for Him, and she saw the risen Jesus. When we find ourselves worrying and weak, we need to evaluate the direction we are moving in; is it our way or God's way?

BATTLE PLAN: Knowing that God equips us with strength when we follow his path is so encouraging. No matter what season of life we are in, we can succeed. When we fall, we pick ourselves up and ask for help. We never quit—no matter what roadblocks are in our way. If we are carrying a backpack full of guilt, low self-esteem, or condemnation, we must leave it on the roadside and keep moving! God is a way maker, and if we are on the trail He wants us to be on, He will provide everything we need and clear the path of any obstacles. It is when we put our trust in God that we can cast away our stone of worry and make great strides toward our goal!

BATTLE SONG: "Way Maker" by Leeland

CAST INTO THE LION'S DEN

"They brought Daniel and cast him into the den of lions. But the king spoke, saying to Daniel, 'Your God, whom you serve continually, he will deliver you' Then the stone was brought and laid on the mouth of the den." —Daniel 6:16-17 (NKJ)

The story of Daniel and the lion's den is written in the Old Testament of the Bible and also in the Jewish Encyclopedia. Daniel (a Jew from the tribe of Judah) was one of King Darius' governors. The king was thinking of putting Daniel in charge of all the governors, so they set out to destroy Daniel. These governors went before the king and told him that there should be an ordinance that states, "anyone who prays to any god or any human being during the next thirty days, except to you, Your Majesty, shall be thrown into the lion's den" (Daniel 6:7 NIV). The king did as the governors requested. The law of land stated that once a king issued a decree, nobody (not even the king) could change it. The governors went to the king and told him that Daniel prayed a few times a day to his god. The king tried everything he could to prevent Daniel from being thrown into the lion's den, but he was unsuccessful. In the morning King Darius rushed to the lion's den to see if Daniel was alive and he was. Daniel told the king, "My God sent his angel, and he shut the mouths of lions. They have not hurt me, because I was found innocent in his sight. Nor have I ever done any wrong to you, Your Majesty" (Daniel 6:22 NIV). The king was so happy that Daniel was alive!

This Daniel is the same Daniel whose friends, Shadrach, Meshach, and Abed-Nego, were thrown into the fiery furnace and the Lord saved them. Perhaps their survival was on Daniel's mind when he was thrown into the lion's den, and he knew that God was more than capable of saving him from the mouths of the lions. Throughout the Old and New Testaments of the Bible, there are countless stories of miraculous events. Yet, people today still doubt God's ability to heal their disease, provide for their needs, or to protect them from evil. God has recently healed people miraculously, so what prevents us from believing that God won't heal us of our infirmities? I believe it is a lack of faith. Even though Jesus said repeatedly while on Earth that we are healed because of our faith, people don't believe it. Perhaps these words that Jesus said will give us the faith we need: "I tell you the truth, anyone who believes in me will do the same works I have done, and even greater works, because I am going to be with the Father. You can ask anything in my name, and I will do it, so that the Son can bring glory to the Father" (John 14:12-13 NLT). Jesus is always interceding for us; our job is to ask and believe.

BATTLE PLAN: God gave us this warning in His word: "Be alert and of sober mind. Your enemy the devil prowls around like a roaring lion looking for someone to devour" (1 Peter 5:8 NIV). Charles Spurgeon said, *"Christ's people must have bold, unflinching lion-like hearts, loving Christ first, and His truth next, and Christ and His truth beyond all the world."* Satan wants to kill and destroy, and God wants to heal and restore. Therefore, we should be bold and not back down from the enemy's' attacks, while believing and trusting in God's promises. When we cry out to Jesus, He will intercede for us and help us win the battle!

BATTLE SONG: "You Are I Am" by MercyMe

CASTING AWAY SHARKS

"God said, Let us make man in our image, after our likeness: and let them have dominion over the fish of the sea" —Genesis1:26 (KJV)

In August of 2015, I was visiting a friend in the Outer Banks of North Carolina. We both love to go to the beach and a few people had been attacked by sharks in the weeks prior to my visit. On Sunday, we went to church and there was a pastor from Russia preaching. His message was on Genesis 1 and when he mentioned verse 26 (the opening quote), it really resonated with me. I felt that God was reminding me of His power in me. After the service I asked my friend if we could go to the beach, get in the water, and command the sharks to leave in Jesus' name and she said yes!

When we arrived at the beach there were many people there. My friend and I had dresses on, and we were laughing because people were going to think we were crazy going into the water dressed like that. The waves were crashing pretty close to shore, so we walked into the water until we were about knee-deep. We closed our eyes and I prayed with authority out loud, *"In the name of Jesus Christ I command any sharks that are in these waters to leave the coast now and go out to sea."* As we walked out of the water in our wet dresses, people were staring at us. We went back to my friend's house and changed into our bathing suits and headed back to the beach.

My daughter was vacationing up the coast with her friends and she called me and told me that she was sitting at the beach facing the water and people were running out of the water as a couple of sharks were swimming by them heading away from the coast. I told her that was because I had gotten in the water and told them to leave in Jesus' name. She said, *"What?!"* I then explained the series of events that prompted me to do that. I asked her what time the sharks swam by her, and the timing made sense in conjunction with my prayer. There were no shark attacks for the rest of the week. In fact, there were no attacks in the area for the rest of the summer. There certainly is power in the name of Jesus!!

This doesn't mean that Jesus is like a genie who must grant our wishes. What we ask God for has to line up with His word and His will; we also must have faith that He will do it. The Bible says that man has authority over the fish in the sea, and I took that scripture literally and told the sharks to leave. I have also prayed many other things in Jesus' name and God has answered my prayers. If you are a Christian, I hope you realize that the power of the Holy Spirit resides in you. Therefore, use the weapon of prayer to defeat the enemy of despair!

BATTLE PLAN: When we pray with faith believing our prayers will be answered, it is amazing what God can/will do. We often limit Him with our unbelief. For example, if my daughter was trying to get an appointment with someone I knew, who happened to be very famous, I would tell her to mention my name when she called. If my daughter did not believe that I really knew that person or didn't mention my name on the call, she is the one that prevented me from helping her. It is so important for people to read and know God's word, so that they can claim all the promises that God has for them. Most parents would not tell their children that they will do something that they cannot do. Jesus said, "If you sinful people know how to give good gifts to your children, how much more will your heavenly Father give good gifts to those who ask Him!" (Matthew 7:11 NLT). Believe in the promises of God and do not limit the possibilities He has for you!

BATTLE SONG: "Faith" by Hillsong Worship

GATHERING PRECIOUS STONES FROM HIDDEN TREASURES

"I will give you treasures hidden in the darkness—secret riches. I will do this so you may know that I am the Lord." —Isaiah 45:3 (NLT)

Many of us grew up hearing fables of pirates and buried treasures. When I was in elementary school, my friends and I decided to go looking for "jewels." We got on our bikes and stopped at a field and carefully searched the area. Then, we rode up the street where there were some woods and explored the terrain, but we came up empty handed. However, we still believed treasure chests existed, just not where we lived. There are some true stories throughout history where people found gold in rivers, money in attics, and old toys that are worth a fortune today.

The question is: are the things in the paragraph above *really* treasures? Dictionary.com states that they are. The first definition of treasure on their website is "wealth or riches stored or accumulated especially in the form of precious metals, money, jewels, or plate," which paints a picture of "things." We can agree that people do need money to pay for shelter, clothing, and food, but that sounds more like a necessity, rather than a treasure. The third definition of treasure is listed as, "anything or person greatly valued or highly prized," which indicates something/someone of value. Yet, the fifth definition of treasure written is, "to regard or treat as precious; cherish." Some people treat their cars or other material things as "precious," while others think of their children as "precious."

In the scripture quoted above it says that treasure is given, so that we will know who God is. It also states that *"it is hidden in darkness."* One of my favorite quotes is by Roman Catholic Mystic Madam Guyon: "I have learned to love the darkness of sorrow for it is there I see the brightness of God's face." It is in the midnight hour, our darkest moments, and during our deepest sorrow that we are desperate for a savior—times when money, possessions, and people cannot solve our dilemma. Sadly, it is usually when all else fails that we turn to God and pray for help. It is there that we will find a real treasure—a heavenly Father waiting to be welcomed into our life, so that He can shower us with His blessings. It was during the worst times of my life that I learned so much about God and His "secret riches" of unconditional love, peace, and comfort. The "brightness of God's face," was a lighthouse in the raging seas that guided me back to shore where I found healing and peace. He was the anchor that kept my mind from drifting away to a place of hopelessness and fear. His steady chains of love held me and brought me stability and confidence, so that I could face whatever the next storm brought into my life. Which definition fits your description of "treasure," and who or what do you consider precious?

BATTLE PLAN: The riches that God offers are treasures that all the money in the world cannot buy. "We have this treasure in earthen vessels, that the excellence of the power may be of God and not of us" (2 Corinthians 4:7). It is often through the sorrow of loss and the fear of cancer that we learn to love the darkness, because we realize who God truly is—someone to *"cherish"* who is *"precious"* and *"highly valued."* Matthew 6:21(NIV) says, "For where your treasure is, there your heart will be also." As a child, I searched for a buried treasure and found it as an adult! It took so long to find because I was searching in the wrong place; I never thought that sorrow was the map to my treasure. If you are still looking for your treasure you can find it easily—it is where your heart is!

BATTLE SONG: "Broken Vessels (Amazing Grace)" by Hillsong

CASTING AWAY OUR IDOLS

"Dear children, keep away from anything that might take God's place in your hearts."—1 John 5:21 (NLT)

Hurricanes are so dangerous because conditions can change suddenly. Meteorologists warn us when one is approaching, but sometimes the damage is much less or much worse than they imagined. Even after storms are over, high tides and river overflows can cause catastrophic damage because the flood waters keep rising for days. Sadly, some people lose their lives, while others survive—it is safe to say that we cannot anticipate what the future brings.

It was during my daughter's junior year in high school when a metaphorical hurricane appeared. My husband and I were separated, but I felt that I had everything under control. My daughter was taking the necessary tests to prepare for her college applications, and we were visiting universities. After eating a piece of cake at a birthday party she developed a rash. I brought my daughter to the doctor, and he put her on prednisone for a week to stop the allergic reaction. The rash appeared to be going away and I thought we had gone through the worst part of the "hurricane." However, like the waters start rising after a storm, my daughter started getting more symptoms. She developed another type of rash and started having high fevers. I was constantly bringing her to the ER and one day, I took her to a different hospital and she was admitted. Her blood work showed that she was very sick. The waters from the flood had risen to dangerous levels. Her spleen was enlarged, her kidneys were not functioning well, she had several rashes, and her temperature was very high and would not go down. I slept in her hospital room every night, people were praying, and I was crying out to the Lord constantly for her healing. The doctors were testing her for all different diseases and the results were coming back normal, but her condition was getting worse. There were ten infectious disease doctors working on her case and they couldn't figure out what was wrong, so they diagnosed her with something that I found out later was a misdiagnosis.

I did not know what to pray for anymore. One night while my daughter was sleeping, I had a talk with God. I was literally crying, asking Him why He was allowing this and what did He want me to do? A thought came to my mind that I needed to surrender my daughter to Him—I told God that He could take her home to heaven if He wanted too. The next day she started showing improvement and she was discharged later that week. God showed me that my daughter was my God, not Him. She was my everything, my idol. I would sing in church "I surrender all" to God, but I didn't. It was through this storm, with its rising floodwaters, that I really had to trust God with my daughter's life. It was through letting go of her that I was able to keep her.

BATTLE PLAN: "When you cry out for help, let your collection of idols save you. The wind will carry all of them off, a mere breath will blow them away. But he whoever takes refuge in me will inherits the land" (Isaiah 57:13 NIV). Is there something or someone in your life right now that takes the place of God? If you find yourself surrounded by the rising waters and all looks hopeless, cry out to God, let go, and trust Him. He promises that the rising waters will not overflow you and that He will be with you (Isaiah 43:2 KJV). When you cast away your idol—that thing that you think you can't live without, or the person that is your god—you will finally be free from the bondage of fear and live the life God intended you to have.

BATTLE SONG: "Let Go, Let God" by Jack Cassidy

DON'T CAST AWAY YOUR PEARLS OF TIME

"Do not give dogs what is sacred; do not throw your pearls to pigs. If you do, they may trample them under their feet, and turn and tear you to pieces —Matthew 7:6 (NIV)

Time is something that cannot be retrieved once it is lost. We have no control over the amount of time that is in an hour, a day, or a year. However, we can control what we do with our time. Jesus said, "Don't store up treasures here on earth, where moths eat them and rust destroys them, and where thieves break in and steal" (Matthew 6:19 NLT). Our time is often spent finding a person, or a thing that will make us happy. However, sometimes when we give away the pearls (pieces) of our treasure (heart) to people or things that are not deserving of it, we get trampled by betrayal, pain, and suffering. Restringing whatever is left of the scattered pearls is difficult; the time spent reconstructing the torn pieces of our lives is lost. In fact, sometimes we waste more time trying to piece everything together by ourselves, rather than asking God for help and guidance.

When we look for people to fill the emptiness inside of us, and we spend our time searching for that "perfect" someone to take away the hurt and loneliness, we are putting our expectations in the wrong place. We must ask ourselves: *can I always do the right thing to keep someone happy and NEVER let them down?* That is a tall order for anyone to fill and I would never want that responsibility because I know it would be impossible for me to do. Yet, we often believe that lie that Satan dangles in front us, I know I did. It is during these times that we need to remember that God can give us a new heart and put a new spirit within it (Ezekiel 36:26 KJV). I know this promise to be true because God healed my heart after my divorce from my first marriage of twenty-one years, and after the death of my second husband.

While seeking God's will for my life, I had the desire to go back to school, which opened up a whole new world to me. Someone I knew at the time asked, "Why are you spending your time studying, why not look for a husband?" My answer was, "Because I discovered that people cannot make me happy, nor is it their responsibility to fill the emptiness in my heart. I learned that searching for happiness is truly like looking for a needle in a haystack. However, pursuing what God created us to be, brings a peace and joy that no human can provide." Where is your time spent and what pearls are you casting before swine?

BATTLE PLAN: When we seek God and His will, He not only heals our broken hearts (Psalm 147:3 KJV), but He also gives purpose to our lives. Psalm 37:4 (KJV) says, "Delight thyself also in the LORD, and he shall give thee the desires of thine heart. Commit thy way unto the Lord, and He shall bring it to pass." You are a precious gem in God's eyes, and He has a plan and purpose for your life—but you need to believe this about Him and yourself. Once you decide to seek God's will, be on guard because the enemy of your soul wants to keep you depressed and searching for happiness in all the wrong places. He is a liar and a thief who wants to trample your dreams and tear you to pieces. He may even dangle people in your path to lead you astray. Psalm 37 says to commit our way to the Lord. When we do this, God aligns His desires with our desires. Our time is no longer spent pursuing things that lead to disappointment, but rather pursing the things we were created to accomplish, which fills us with joy. Then, if God wants to put someone in our path He will, and it will be a match made in heaven!

BATTLE SONG: "You've Always Been" by Unspoken

Cast Away Stones of Unforgiveness, Gather Stones of Peace

"Get rid of all bitterness, rage and anger, harsh words and slander, as well as all types of evil behavior. Instead, be kind to each other, tenderhearted, forgiving one another, just as God through Christ has forgiven you." —Ephesians 4:31-32 (NLT)

Why is that we can forgive others, but we have such a hard time forgiving ourselves? C.S. Lewis said, "I think that if God forgives us, we must forgive ourselves. Otherwise, it is almost like setting up ourselves as a higher tribunal than him." Lewis' quote makes sense; denying self-forgiveness causes us to concentrate on ourselves, some may say it is a form of pride. When the enemy sees this breach in our obedience to God, he fires a round of regret and throws grenades of self-condemnation into our mind. When they explode, they trigger certain scenarios in our thoughts: *If I had only kept my mouth shut; if I did what I promised I would do; if I had defended my friend; if I was there when they needed me.* When this takes place the enemy of our soul has us right where he wants us: self-absorbed. When we are in this state, we are not engaged in life and therefore, out of the battle. I can almost hear him playing the song, "Another One Bites the Dust."

We have all had times in our lives when we have said or done something that we regret. The Bible says that there is "no condemnation to them which are in Christ Jesus, who walk not after the flesh, but after the Spirit" (Romans 8:1 KJV). So, after we repent and ask God to forgive us and apologize to the person we offended, we need to let it go. If we do not, this guilt can present itself in the form of anger, resentment, or unkindness; sometimes these emotions show up at the most inappropriate times. We cannot change the past, but we can move forward and have a promising future.

BATTLE PLAN: When we take our proper place and let God be God, He will help us overcome our despair. "For as high as the heavens are

147

above the earth, so great is his love for those who fear him; as far as the east is from the west, so far has he removed our transgressions from us" (Psalm 103:12-13 NIV). Once we grab hold of this precious gift from God, our stones of depression will disappear. The breach will be closed, the enemy defeated, and we can begin to gather stones of peace.

BATTLE SONG: "Come as You Are" by David Crowder

A TIME TO EMBRACE, AND A TIME TO REFRAIN FROM EMBRACING—ECCLESIASTES 3:5B

EMBRACING ADVERSITY & RISING ABOVE THE STORM

*"In the third month, the sun rising, the Boar and the Leopard on the field of Mars to fight; the tired Leopard raises its eye to the heavens, sees an eagle **playing around the sun**."* —Nostradamus

D o you know that eagles are fearless and they like storms? Instead of flying away from the approaching tempest, like other birds do, they use the gale force winds to lift them up above the clouds. Even when the weather is normal, they tap into the breezes and use their large wingspan to glide for miles. Their powerful long wings are light, which helps them soar even faster and farther. I believe that God wants us to face the storms in life like the eagles do: using the overpowering wind to our advantage. So, what prevents us from doing this? It's fear.

When we trust God and face the elements of life's trials, rather than run from them, He can lift us up above the clouds. "Like an eagle that stirs up its nest, that hovers over its young, He spread His wings and caught them. He carried them on His pinions" (Deuteronomy 32:11 NLT). God will catch us too when we fall; He never expects us to face the tempest alone. He promises to be with us; "Have I not commanded you? Be strong and courageous. Do not be afraid; do not be discouraged, for the LORD your God will be with you wherever you go" (Joshua 1:9 NIV). When we run away from the approaching storm, like birds other than eagles do, we miss blessings that were intended for us. God wants us **playing around the sun** enjoying its warmth during the storm. When we tap into the Holy Spirit's guidance, we can glide above the storm.

Are you exhaustingly battling the strong winds of adversity like the leopard? If so, why not be like the eagle and embrace the gale. God promises that "those who trust in the Lord find new strength. They will soar high and on wings like eagles, they will run and not grow weary, they will walk and not faint" (Isaiah 40:31 NLT). Notice how the scripture says those who "trust"—putting our faith and trust in God is necessary to overcome the powerful storms in life.

BATTLE PLAN: God will never send a trial our way unless He has a purpose for it. Just like the mother eagle throw's her young out of the nest, so they can learn how to fly, God pushes us out of our comfort zone, so that we can fly through the face of fear and accomplish our life's mission. Watching an eagle soar is a beautiful sight. It's amazing how it grabs hold of the wind, which enables it to effortlessly glide for miles at high speeds. This is how it will be when we put our trust in our heavenly Father. We will grab hold of the winds and fly through the tribulation, soaring above the clouds and playing around the sun. People will watch in amazement and be inspired to soar themselves.

BATTLE SONG: "Like Eagles" by Don Moen

EMBRACE THE OFFER

"Everything the world offers comes with an expiration date." —Alex Adamapoulos

If you watch TV, listen to the radio, or shop at stores, you will notice that every offer or sale price has an expiration date. A sale sometimes entices consumers to buy things that they don't need now, because the price is good. When COVID reared its fearful face, people were stocking up on groceries that had expiration dates years away.

It is no secret that manufacturers use advertising strategies that manipulate your mind; their goal is to convince you that you need to purchase the product being advertised. As such, people put their hope in products that will make them look younger, feel better, or entertain them. Some of these items come with a warranty, which assures the purchaser that the company will cover the cost of the parts needed to restore the product to its original condition.

Merchandise and warranties are not the only things that have timeframes. People often give someone a certain time limit: to apologize, to change their bad behavior, or to commit to a relationship. If the deadline hits and the demands have not been met—the relationship is over. However, God's forgiveness and salvation offer don't expire because it doesn't depend on our performance, but rather on His unconditional love. There is no manipulation used to get you to accept His offer and it is available until you take your last breath.

The extended warranty carries you into eternity. In heaven everything will be freely provided and there will be nothing that we desire. Our bodies won't need beauty products or medicine because we will have new bodies that will be perfect. We won't need self-help books or entertainment to get our minds off our broken hearts because there will be no more tears in heaven. You really can't beat this offer— it will be the best purchase you will ever make. Since God's expiration date aligns with the expiration of your life, don't wait to embrace this offer!

BATTLE PLAN: When Jesus walked this earth, He healed many people. A father brought his son to Jesus to be healed and Jesus told him that "Anything is possible if a person believes" (Mark 9:23 NLT). Then he asked the father if he believed and his response was, "Lord, I do believe; but help me overcome my unbelief!" (Mark 9:24 NLT). Jesus healed the man's son. Many people in the world today want proof that God exists and His son Jesus died for our sins. Actually, you can find proof on the history channel that Jesus actually did exist, was crucified, died, and was buried. The bible states that many people saw the resurrected Jesus after the crucifixion. Satan's plan is to convince people that when they die, they will be able to plead their case to God and enter heaven, but it does not work that way. You must accept Jesus' gift of salvation before you die. If you want to believe that God exists and there is a heaven, but are having a hard time believing it, do what the father did in the story in Mark 9: tell the Lord you believe and ask Him to help you with your unbelief. God will show you that He is real. I know this because God loves you and His word says, "If you look for me wholeheartedly, you will find me" (Jeremiah 29:13 NLT). The enemy will do everything he can to keep you from accepting the gift of salvation. This is one battle you must win; once you accept God's invitation for salvation, you are His and He will fight for you. If you are already a Christian, stay in the fight and keep persevering until the Lord takes you home.

BATTLE SONG: "Great Expectations" by Steven Curtis Chapman

Embracing God's Answer

"For the LORD God is a sun and a shield; the LORD gives grace and glory; no good thing will he withhold from them that walk uprightly." —Psalm 84:11 (KJV)

Some people believe that God always answers prayers. However, that doesn't mean that the answer is always yes; sometimes it's no, or not yet. The sun can be both beneficial and destructive. Without the sun, life could not exist; however, too much sun can cause cancer, heatstroke, and possibly death. As such, it is essential that we know and understand the consequences of both the good and the bad.

Sometimes when we really want something, our perception of whether it is best for us may be a little skewed because we are only looking at the positive aspects of it, and how much we want it. Perhaps we do not even realize how dangerous it could be. Afterall, people underestimate the damage that the sun can cause all the time.

When my daughter was in high school, computers were getting popular and she wanted one; she was and still is an overachiever. My reply to her request was no, you can go to the library and use the computer there, even though I could have easily afforded a computer. Her sunny disposition was soon downcast. She didn't realize that I was trying to shield her from the dangers lurking in the world, and that she could find herself in a vulnerable situation.

Many months later my daughter planned to go to the library on the weekend to work on a research paper that was due on Monday. However, the meteorologist said that a snowstorm was heading our way. As such, I decided that I would buy her a computer. I knew that my daughter would act responsibly, but I decided to put the computer in my office, so that I could monitor what she was doing and protect her as much as possible from online predators. God loves us just as much as we love our children, if not more. The difference is He knows exactly where the dangers are and knows the plans of our enemy. If your prayers have not been answered, perhaps God is protecting you from danger that you cannot see. In times like this, trust that God knows what He is doing. He may not give you want you want, but He will always give you what you need.

BATTLE PLAN: There is a song by Garth Brooks called "Unanswered Prayers," which is about a man that prayed for someone to be his wife, but his prayer was not answered. In the song the man is thanking God for the unanswered prayer because the woman he ended up marrying was a perfect match for him. One of the definitions of the word *embrace* is, "to accept something willingly or gladly." Whatever you are currently praying for, *embrace* God's answer to your request— He definitely knows and wants what is best for you! He will never withhold anything good from us, unless He is trying to protect us from something. God may also withhold things from us teach us a lesson, because we are walking through life without Him, and He is trying to get our attention. During times like this, the enemy will whisper in your ear that God doesn't want you to be happy; however, Satan is the one who wants to see you suffer, not God! Don't fall for the enemy's lies.

BATTLE SONG: "Good Good Father" by Chris Tomlin

REFRAIN FROM EMBRACING THE ENEMY'S TRAPS

"Every moment of resistance to temptation is a victory." —*Theologian Frederick William Faber*

A ddiction is a weapon that the devil and human beings have been using for thousands of years. When the British took control of India in the eighteenth century, they gained access to the opium fields in India. They began selling opium to China and the Chinese people got addicted to it. China tried to stop the opium from coming into their country, but Britain continued to smuggle opium into China, which led to the Opium Wars. The Bible states that "the love of money is a root of all kinds of evil" (1 Timothy 6:10 NIV). There are many reasons why people sell drugs, but the main reason is probably money. We know that Satan is behind the evil in the world (1 John 5:19), but money means nothing to him. He is after the souls of human beings, and he uses money to get people to commit his evil deeds.

Some Chinese people who immigrated to America in the late eighteen hundreds introduced Americans to opium. Today, a variety of dangerous drugs enter the American border daily, and there is a huge drug addiction problem in the United States and in other countries as well. Many people throughout the world have gotten addicted to opioids because of an injury, while other people became addicted to psychiatric medication because of trauma, depression, or postpartum depression. Drugs are not the only thing that people can become addicted to; they can also become addicted to alcohol, video games, food, and other behaviors. If you are currently struggling with addiction, God wants to free you from it! The enemy wants to kill and destroy you, and God wants to heal you and give you an abundant life. Remember God is with you, but He has given you free will so you must ask for His help and make the decision to resist temptation.

BATTLE PLAN: The enemy wants you to think that you cannot win the battle of addiction, but you can! As Frederick Faber said in the opening quote, it is every MOMENT of resisting temptation that secures our victory. The apostle Paul said, "The temptations in your life are no different from what others experience. And God is faithful. He will not allow the temptation to be more than you can stand. When you are tempted, he will show you a way out so that you can endure" (1 Corinthians 10:13-14 NLT). God will help you fight the temptation from the enemy, but you have to seek and ask for his help. When He shows you a way out, embrace it!

BATTLE SONG: "Chain Breaker" by Zach Williams

EMBRACING GOD'S FRAGRANCE

"The fragrance of His knowledge."— *2 Corinthians 2:14*

There are all kinds of fragrances in the world that serve different purposes. Some are used to cover up fowl scents, while others are used to ward off predators. Yet, what often smells good to some people, does not smell good to other people. Lavender has a nice aroma and is used for many things. Its soothing scent helps relax people that have anxiety, and those who are unable to sleep because they suffer from insomnia. However, if lavender is planted in a vegetable garden it acts as a repellent for deer because they hate the smell.

When I was young and didn't get up in time to take a shower before leaving for school, I would put on perfume to cover up any body odor. This strategy actually worked until it wore off. The opening scripture means that if we truly know Christ, we should have the same aroma that He does. Therefore, if we have "knowledge of Him" and His ways, we are supposed to live according to them, so that others will smell His scent of love, forgiveness, compassion, and peace when they are around us. People, however, can often cover up their true fragrance for a while; they are loving and kind until you disagree with them, they have compassion for you until you ignore their advice, and they preach grace until you hurt their feelings. Jesus, however, loves sacrificially, has immense compassion, and forgives those who sin against Him.

In the world of fragrance, a knock off brand is made with cheaper ingredients or synthetic ones, and also lacks longevity. Similarly, people who know God's word, but do not know Him intimately will fall apart quickly when they are faced with a trial. Seriously, how can you put your hope and trust in someone you don't really know. Even if we have a great personal relationship with the Lord, we can still fall short of His glory. The Bible says that, "There is none righteous, no, not one" (Romans 3:10 KJV). God knows that no matter how hard we try to emulate Jesus, we are going to fail sometimes. When we do, we need to repent of our actions, ask God and those we hurt for forgiveness, and let Him take all the synthetic scents of the world out of us so that He can fill us with His sweet aroma.

BATTLE PLAN: What type of fragrance fills the room when you walk in? Does it attract people to you, or repel them away? If you are there for a while does the scent begin to evaporate because you haven't been filled with God's sweet aroma of love, peace, and joy? If so, we need to ditch the imitation aroma and be who we really are. When we are honest with ourselves, God has access to work in our hearts and turn us into the wonderful fragrance we were created to be.

BATTLE SONG: "Relate" by for King & Country

EMBRACING YOUR CROSS

"Do not pity me for my blindness for the first face I see will be the face of my Lord Jesus." —Fanny Crosby

Fanny was a famous poet and hymn writer who became blind when she was six weeks old. From her own darkness she brought light, joy, and encouragement to others. She attended a school for the blind and became a teacher at that same institution. Jesus said, "I am the Light of the world; he that followeth me shall not walk in darkness but shall have the light of life" (John 8:12 KJV). When we follow the path that God has for us, He illuminates the way that leads to His will.

Fanny's life was certainly filled with the light of Jesus. I know this because I see the fruit that she produced throughout her time on Earth; it was full of nutrients and minerals. Her Hymns protected the soul from being damaged and brought spiritual vitamins that allowed people to grow. Her teachings produced minerals that kept her students' brains, hearts, bones, and muscles strong, so that they could not only persevere, but they could also use the gifts they had inside of them to make a difference in the world.

There is an old story which you may have already heard. A person was crying out to God saying that their cross was too hard to bear and asked God if they could trade it in for another cross. God agreed and opened the door to a room full of crosses. The person found the smallest cross and said, "I will take this one." God replied, "My dear child, that is the cross you traded in."

We all go through periods in our lives when we feel that we cannot carry our burdens any longer. The best thing for us to do is to ask for God to lighten our load, but sometimes his answer is "my grace is sufficient for thee: for my strength is made perfect in weakness" (2 Corinthians 12:9 NKJ). At times like this, we need to get our eyes off of ourselves and our problems and realize that our cross might just be the smallest one in the room and things could always be worse. Then we need to ask the Lord to give us the strength we need to keep going.

BATTLE PLAN: Fanny had a good reason to trade her cross in for a different one, however, she chose to keep it and accept her blindness. She used the gifts she had to make a difference in the lives of others. She also wrote thousands of Hymns to honor God. I cannot imagine the attacks she received from Satan throughout her life. I'm sure he fired darts of self-pity and discouragement at her. However, by the looks of her accomplishments, the enemy was not successful. We can have that same victory because God promises to give us the strength we need, but we must make the decision to accept that strength and keep persevering like Fanny Crosby did. If we do, God can use our weaknesses to be a light that strengths and teaches others. We all have something we can offer God and others so, let's stay in the fight and win the battle!

BATTLE SONG: "Offering" by Third Day

Embracing God's Guidance

"Coincidences are God's way of staying anonymous." —*Alex Adamopoulos*

In the past, God has often provided help for me when I needed to find someplace; there have been many instances where people would appear out of nowhere. When my daughter graduated college, I took her to Italy to see her boyfriend who was studying abroad. He was traveling from Rome to Florence, from Florence to Verona, and from Verona to Venice. I booked hotels at all those places and my daughter and I traveled by train to each one. It was my first trip to Europe, so I was counting on God to be my guide.

When we were on the train heading to Venice, I had no idea where to go once we arrived. I started praying that God would send someone to help us. When we arrived at the train station, I was looking at a map and trying to find our hotel on it. A man that worked at the station asked if I needed help and I said, "Yes, I do not know what water taxi to take to our hotel." The man kindly told me what taxi I should take and where to get it. When we boarded the boat, I began talking with a couple of people onboard. They said Venice was like a maze, and it could be difficult to navigate. When we arrived at our stop, we got off the boat and had no idea which way to go. Suddenly, a woman appeared out of nowhere and asked me, "Do you need help?" I replied, "Yes, I do not know how get to this hotel" and showed her my reservations. She said that it was about a fifteen-minute walk, and she would be happy to take us there. My daughter and I looked at each other in awe and thanked her profusely. I never would have found our hotel without her help. My prayers were answered, and I was so grateful!

Years later, my daughter was very sick with Lyme disease and some of the antibiotics she had been on for seventeen months were no longer working. She needed a PICC line put in so that she could receive IV antibiotics. When we arrived at the hospital on the day of her procedure I asked her, "Where do we need to go?" and she said, "I don't know, they never told me when I registered, and the doctor never mentioned it either." When we went to the information desk, we found a senior citizen working there. My daughter asked where she would go to have a PICC line put in and he had no idea what she was talking about. No matter how many ways we tried to explain what a PICC line was, he had no idea what we were talking about. While we were conversing, a woman dressed in scrubs walked by and said, "Can I help you find something?" My daughter and I both said "YES!" and explained our situation. She said, "Follow me, I think I know how to get you there." My daughter and I looked at each other and said, "Venice." God has come through for me many times since then. He is the best compass we can ever have!

BATTLE PLAN: In Venice I prayed for God to send someone, but at the hospital, He sent someone before I asked Him for help. Has that ever happened to you? Some people would call that a coincidence or luck. If that is true, what or who is causing this phenomenon? I believe it is our Heavenly Father helping us. God promises in His word that He will show us the path of life (Psalm 16:11 KJV). Traveling from place to place is part of life's journey. Once we embrace God's gift of salvation, we will see His hand in everything! When we take a wrong turn and find ourselves traveling down a path we never intended to be on, or we find ourselves at a crossroads, we will either feel God's spirit saying, "This is the way; walk in it" (Isaiah 30:21 NIV) or He will send someone to help us. We never have to fear because God is always with us.

BATTLE SONG: "Next to Me" by Jordan Feliz

164

EMBRACING YOUR CIRCUMSTANCES

*"I have **learned** to be content whatever the circumstances. I know what it is to be in need, and I know what it is to have plenty. I have **learned** the secret of being content in any and every situation, whether well fed or hungry, whether living in plenty or in want." —Phil 4:11-12 (NIV)*

People learn in different ways and there are many learning styles: visual, auditory, and kinesthetic are the primary ones. While some people can listen to a teaching and comprehend the concepts, some need to see the concept written out, and yet others must physically carry out the activities of the concept. The apostle Paul learned how to be content through experiencing and surviving hunger, physical pain, imprisonment, illness, and poverty.

Paul, who was known as Saul of Tarsus before he became a follower of Christ, was an educated man, a Pharisee, as well as a Roman citizen. There is speculation that his family may have been wealthy. As such, Paul also knew what it was like to not want for anything. One would wonder how a person could go from that lifestyle to the total opposite side of the spectrum and find contentment. According to the world's standards, Paul should have been the happiest when he was Saul.

We often hear stories of people surviving incredible odds, performing impossible feats, or surviving without food for weeks. Their ability to persevere beyond all they could have ever imagined changes their perspective of life and of themselves. For Saul of Tarsus, it was his encounter with Jesus on the road to Damascus, where he traded in his life of prominence, and the privileges that accompanied it, for a life of servanthood to his Savior.

The work that Paul did for the kingdom of God became his passion and life's mission. Someone who serves their country abroad understands the devotion and discipline it takes to be so committed. Paul's missionary trips ended when he was thrown into prison. Nevertheless, he learned to be content in a cell, as well. He had the ability to see life the way that God did; the guards and prisoners in jail became his new mission field and purpose. What an example Paul is for us. If we are not content right now, perhaps God is trying to teach us something.

BATTLE PLAN: As long as we breathe, we can fulfill a purpose in this world. God has given us all special gifts and it is not entirely our title, job, or finances that define who we are—it is our worth in Christ that does. As such, let's not assume that the best part of our lives is over when in fact, it may just be beginning. Jesus said, "He who findeth his life shall lose it, and he who loseth his life for my sake shall find it" (Matthew 10:39 KJV). When life is all about us, we will never be satisfied. The newest things will eventually bore us, nothing will seem to entertain us, and we will eventually realize that all our money can't buy true happiness. When we live our life for God, He will equip us with everything we need for the journey, including peace in the storm, courage for the battle, and strength to continue. Have you learned the secret of being content whatever the circumstances? If not, ask God to help you; He knows your learning style because He created you. God will lovingly guide and encourage you when you embrace the circumstances He has set before you.

BATTLE SONG: "Bring the Rain" by MercyMe

EMBRACING THE WIND

"God never forces a person's will into surrender, and He never begs. He patiently waits until that person willingly yields to Him." —*Oswald Chambers*

Faith is the wind that blows the sailboat, without it, the boat cannot be controlled and is at the mercy of the currents in the ocean. When I was a teenager I learned about the wind, boats, and God the hard way; even though I did not have a relationship with God—He kept me safe. When I was fourteen years old, I spent my summer going to the local beach with my friends. One of my friends had a small sailboat and we all decided to sail to one of the islands off the coast. We piled into the boat and totally disregarded the maximum number of people the boat was equipped for. We made it safely to the island and had a blast exploring it!

On the way back to the mainland the wind picked up and the waves were getting bigger. We decided to all sit on one side of the boat to keep it from tipping over; however, a strong gale came from the opposite side causing the boat to turn over. We landed in the water under the boat and thankfully, we were able to untangle ourselves from the ropes and surface to the top of the water. None of us had lifejackets on, so we held onto the tipped boat and as we looked around there was no land in sight. We were in the water for a while and it was really cold, so I started to silently pray and asked God to send a boat to help us. Not too long after my prayer, a boat came into our sight, and we started screaming to get their attention. They spotted us and drove over to where we were. The boat they were in was not big enough for all of us to fit on so they radioed the Coast Guard and gave them our location; we were told that the Coast Guard would leave immediately to come and get us. It took them a while to get to us and by the time they arrived we were suffering from hypothermia. We all learned the importance of following the rules and guidelines that day. Even when we mess up and disregard "the rules" we should never be afraid to cry out to God!

BATTLE PLAN: Life is full of laws, regulations, and standards that must be obeyed. As citizens, employees, or students there are consequences for not following the rules. It is the same with Christianity as well, except God's laws are based on His love for us, just like earthly parents do for their kids. God sets the bar for blessings or curses; the choice is ours to embrace the requirements or to reject them. However, as humans, we are far from perfect and we are all going to make mistakes. Many of us like to test the waters and not just accept what we are told. The famous author C.S. Lewis made it his goal to prove that there was no God and Christianity was a myth; however, his research proved that the Bible was true and he *"yielded his will to God."* Lewis went on to be a great warrior for God's kingdom and wrote many best-seller books. If we find ourselves capsized somewhere or being pulled by the currents of this world, we should pray for help. God is patiently waiting for us to allow Him into our lives, so that He can not only save us from going under, but also help us charter our course through life.

BATTLE SONG: "Right Here" by Jeremy Camp

A TIME TO GAIN, AND A TIME TO LOSE—ECCLESIASTES 3:6A

LOSING CONTROL

"If God is your co-pilot, swap seats." —James W. Moore

Being in control of our health, finances, relationships, and surroundings gives us a sense of security. Since God gave us free will, we can accomplish these tasks in any way we choose to. The apostle Paul said, "I have the right to do anything…but not everything is beneficial. I have the right to do anything—but I will not be mastered by anything" (1 Corinthians 6:12 NIV). We are told that some things are good for us in moderation: certain foods, alcohol, or shopping are a few of these things. However, abuse of any of them can lead to addiction and I believe that is what Paul is talking about in this scripture when he mentions "mastered by anything."

Jesus was tempted in every way possible while on Earth and He understands how temptation can be relentless. Therefore, He told His disciples, "Watch and pray, that ye enter not into temptation: the spirit indeed is willing, but the flesh weak" (Matthew 26:41 KJV). This is why many of us make New Year's Resolutions that we can never fulfill. Sometimes we are doing well with our diets until we are hit with bad news, or we get hurt by a loved one. We tell ourselves that *it's okay to indulge because it will relieve our stress and make us feel better.* It usually does for a short period of time, until we start feeling guilty for giving in to our desires. Let's face it, life can be a journey of crash diets, and ups and downs. One minute we are flying on course, and then the next minute we hit unexpected turbulence. So, what's a person to do?

One of the most important things we need to do when struggling with an addiction is to admit the fact that we have no control over our fleshly desires. Then we need to make sure that there is somebody in our lives that will hold us accountable for our actions. Once those things are in place, we are prepared to taxi down the runway and takeoff to our destination of deliverance.

The pilot is the one in control when flying an airplane; he or she tells the co-pilot what to do and when to do it. Who is the pilot of our lives, is it God or us? Are we afraid to give up control, so we dictate to Him what we want Him to do, or are we humbly surrendering to His control and following His commands? Why do we insist on being the navigator, even when we can't see a clear path ahead of us and have no idea where we are going? When we insist on being the pilot, we not only put our lives in danger, but also the passengers on board with us.

BATTLE PLAN: God tells us: "Incline your ear, and come unto me; hear, and your soul shall live; and I will make an everlasting covenant with you" (Isaiah 55:3 KJV). What unbeneficial things in our lives have taken control of the tiller, so that we cannot navigate a safe landing when our journey is over? God wants to make a contract with us; if we switch seats with Him and let Him be the pilot of our flight path, we can be assured that we will arrive at the right destination when our journey through life ends. Afterall, He created us and the universe, so He knows where all the turbulence is! So, let's take our proper place, follow orders, and enjoy the flight.

BATTLE SONG: "Control" by For King & Country

SURVIVING LIFE'S CURRENTS

"Love is an element which though physically unseen is as real as air or water. It is an acting, living, moving force…it moves in waves and currents like those of the ocean" — Prentice Mulford

Many people find the ocean therapeutic hearing the waves gently crash on the shore, feeling the sun on their body and the sand under their feet. Did you know that there is something called Ocean Therapy that is now helping people with post-traumatic stress disorder (PTSD)? My dad loved the ocean, and I'm sure that Ocean Therapy would have helped him with his PTSD from World War II. My parents had me at the beach at a young age and I learned to swim when I was just a few years old. As a teenager, I swam in rapids at a local beach and water-skied. When I was sixteen, I took the test to get certified as a lifeguard and I use to surf as well. The bigger the waves, the more fun they were to play in. I never felt afraid in the water.

As an adult, I was vacationing with my daughter in the Outer Banks and we were having a blast body surfing in the waves, which were a few feet over my head. Suddenly, I got caught in a rip current and was quickly being pulled out to sea. I tried to swim to the shore and couldn't, then I remembered to swim to the side, and I eventually caught a wave and rode it in. We got out of the water and my respect for the ocean and its power grew tremendously.

Sometimes when you learn about the dangers in life you never take the warning signs seriously; you either think that you are prepared to handle whatever life may throw at you, or you underestimate the danger and your abilities. I was married in my early twenties to a man that could make me laugh even if I was mad at him. He was a great provider and a good person. He fought in the Vietnam War when he was eighteen and I knew he was struggling with what we now know is PTSD. I did not know how to help him, and he did not want to talk about it. I had biblical grounds for divorce, but I kept telling myself that if I could just keep loving him, eventually he would be okay. However, things got worse, and I felt like we were caught in a rip current. For years I tried to get him to swim to the side for help so we could be free of the current, but I was unsuccessful. God was always there encouraging me; He actually used the treacherous waters to bring me closer to Him. After twenty-one years of praying and seeking God for guidance, I knew He wanted me to swim to the side alone and free myself from the exhaustion and struggle to stay afloat, so I did. My ex-husband and I are still friends; he finally got help for his PTSD and last year he married a wonderful woman. Perhaps you are caught in a rip current that you cannot get out of; maybe it's a toxic relationship, an addiction, or a financial disaster. Know that God is in the undercurrent with you and will help if you ask Him to. Seek Him and trust Him!

BATTLE PLAN: God promises, "You will seek me and find me when you seek me with all your heart" (Jeremiah 29:13 NIV). Sometimes God frees us from the current right away; other times it may take a while. However, those years of exhaustingly treading water to stay afloat will never be wasted. He will work them together for your good and the good of others. It is only after we survive the strong pull of the out flowing sea, that we can help others find their way to shore.

Don't fear the dark blue water where the current may be,
What seems to be a curse may be a blessing you see,
The water that is pulling you to places unknown,
May be helping you reach God on His Heavenly throne,
Through total surrender and losing control,
God can take what is broken and make it all whole,
By fighting your fears and using the current for good,
God takes you to places, you never thought He could.

BATTLE SONG: "Oceans" by Hillsong

Discovering the Truth and Gaining Eternal Life

"If false, Christianity is not important. If true, it is of infinite importance. What it cannot be is moderately important." —C.S. Lewis

If anyone could make this opening statement, it was C. S. Lewis. As an atheist he set out to prove that there is no God and that the gospel is not true. Over a decade later, he accepted Jesus Christ as his Savior and surrendered his life to the Him. Ironically, it was Lewis' doubt that led him to the truth, and he became one of the best disciples for God's kingdom.

What was so powerful about Lewis' testimony was that he didn't base his conclusion on his feelings or intellectual thinking, but rather on the evidence he found to be true. 1Thessalonians 5:19 NIV says, "Do not quench the Spirit. Do not treat prophecies with contempt but test them all; hold on to what is good, reject every kind of evil." Anyone who seriously searches for the truth will see that the prophesies regarding Jesus in the Old Testament came true, as well as many other prophetic events. One can look at the events going on in the world today—rumors of war, earthquakes, famine, pestilence, lawlessness, and people being offended (Matthew 24:7-10)—and see that Jesus warned about these things thousands of years ago.

Life and death are realities for every human being. Each one is extremely important in the scheme of things: how we live our lives will determine where we spend eternity. When we stand before God someday, there will be no excuse for the decisions we made. Everyone has the opportunity in their life to seek the truth. God promises that "You will seek me and find me when you seek me with all your heart. I will be found by you declares the LORD and will bring you back from captivity (Jeremiah 29:13-14 NIV). Time on earth is a blink of an eye compared to the endless time of eternity. If we don't know where we are spending eternity, we need to seriously search for the truth because the worst thing we can do is to be dead wrong when we take our last breath!

BATTLE PLAN: Many people take pieces of different religions and blend them together to create a God and a religion that they believe is right in their own mind. Satan loves this because he is the author of that theology. He fooled Eve in the garden of Eden by twisting God's word. In fact, he knows God's word better than many Christians. Some people believe in God and Jesus, but do not believe that Jesus is the only way to get into heaven. If that is true, then why would God send His only Son to suffer and die on a cross for us? I can't imagine watching one of my kids suffer and die such a horrific death for others, if there was another way. If we can get into heaven by being good, who sets the bar on what is good and where can that information be found? It certainly isn't the ten commandments because nobody can keep all of those; everyone has told at least one lie in their lifetime. Jesus said the following two things: "Because you are lukewarm—neither hot nor cold—I am about to spit you out of my mouth" (Revelations 3:16 NIV), and "Whoever is not with me is against me" (Matthew 12:30 NIV). Therefore, it is so important for us to search out the truth ourselves because eternity is forever. Lewis said...pick a side because you can't be neutral! If you have already chosen Jesus, now is the time to keep fighting for His kingdom! If not, what are you waiting for?

BATTLE SONG: "Ready For You" by Kutless

Losing the Grip of the Past & Gaining Control of the Future

"You can't go back and change the beginning, but you can start where you are and change the ending." —C.S. Lewis

We all have skeletons in the closet that try to come out every now and then, things that we wished we never said or did. Regret can be crippling—it steals our joy, keeps us in bondage, and prevents us from moving forward. You may have heard the story about the man who was driving down the street, constantly looking in his review mirror because the car behind him was driving to close to him. He was worried that the car would hit him. Since the man was looking behind while driving, rather than looking forward, he hit the car in front of him.

God purposely put our eyes in the front of our head, so we could see what's ahead of us. Our past is our past, therefore, we can only relive those days in our minds. Reminiscing about the blessings we have received is a good thing, but mulling over our mistakes, shortcomings, and tragedies of the past causes us to relive the pain and suffering all over again. When we do the latter, we are missing out on the present, and the daily blessings and opportunities that God has for us. As such, let's make today the day we break free from the past, so we can enjoy the day.

BATTLE PLAN: Satan's goal is to steal our joy, our peace, and our hope. One of the best ways he can do this is to keep us regretting the past and fearing the future. Regrets cause depression, which takes away our desire to engage in life. Fear has the same outcome because it also prevents us from living in the day and moving forward. God's plan for us is the complete opposite of the enemy's. God's word states, "For I know the thoughts that I think toward you, says the Lord, thoughts of peace and not evil, to give you a future and a hope" (Jeremiah 29:11 NKJ). The decisions we make today impact where we will be tomorrow. Don't let the enemy win—appreciate the present day and be grateful for it, it may not seem like it, but things could always be worse. We must stop believing the lies of the enemy and start embracing the promises of God. Find a scripture in the Bible that encourages you and have it put on your coffee mug; it will be a great reminder each morning to embrace the day, trust God and start living again!

BATTLE SONG: "Tomorrow" by Unspoken

LIVE IN ACTUALITIES

"Submit yourself therefore to God. Resist the devil, and he will flee from you." — *James 4:7 (KJV)*

Sometimes things happen suddenly: an injury, an illness, or a loss. After the initial shock wears off, we find ourselves in unchartered territory, with no map or GPS to guide us. On top of the chaos, we are often bombarded with people giving their unsolicited advice on how we should proceed. As we listen, we are thinking...*you have never been in this situation, and you have no idea what I am going through!* There is, however, someone who truly does understand—Jesus. He experienced everything we will ever go through while He was on this earth.

I think we can all admit that losing control over an area of our life is scary, especially if you are an independent person. God brings us into new seasons of our lives for different reasons: to teach us something, to use us in the future to help others, or to bring us back into relationship with Him. God told the people of Israel, "For a brief moment I abandoned you, but with deep compassion I will bring you back" (Isaiah 54:7 NIV). Even though it was their sinful lifestyle that made God turn His back on them in the first place, He brought them out of captivity. Jesus never said that we wouldn't have trouble, pain, or heartache in our lives, but He did say, "Be of good cheer; I have overcome the world (John16:33 KJV). So, how can we stay optimistic when calamity strikes? We seek God's guidance and believe His promises—then, we resist the thoughts the devil is firing into our minds

The apostle Paul said, "We are troubled on every side, yet not distressed; we are perplexed, but not in despair; persecuted, but not forsaken; cast down, but not destroyed" (2 Corinthians 4:7-9 KJV). If we meditate on these truths and ask the Lord for help, He will provide the strength and wisdom we need to get through each day. King Solomon was known to be the wisest man in the world. He once said, "For as he thinketh in heart, so, is he (Proverbs 23:7 KJV). When we find ourselves in a season of affliction, how do we think and see ourselves? Are we warriors or worriers? Are we trusting or fearing?

We can find these answers easily; we just need to look at what we are meditating on.

BATTLE STRATEGY: Satan has a plan for the spiritual battles we face daily. Part of that plan is to get us to constantly focus on ourselves and our problems, so that we stop engaging in life. However, if we meditate on God's truths, and all the times He has been faithful to get us through our trials in the past, we suddenly feel encouraged, rather than depressed. Therefore, we must not let the enemy trick us into believing that God has abandoned us. Remember, Jesus set us free from bondage—we must fight for that freedom! If we are in a season of blessings right now, we should praise God for that and then pray for those who are being attacked.

BATTLE SONG: "Truth" Is by Danny Gokey

LOSING GUILT, GAINING FREEDOM

"The Lord looks down from heaven and sees the whole human race. From his throne he observes all who live on the earth. He made their hearts, so he understands everything they do." —Psalm 33:13-15 (NLT)

Have you ever done or said something that you wish you could take back? In golf, you might have the chance to take a "mulligan," which allows you to retake a lousy shot. In society today, there is a thing called "cancel culture" that expels someone from society if they have ever said or did something offensive to anyone in their life. It doesn't matter how long ago it was, how old you were at the time, what the norm was during that era, or if you have even apologized for your wrong actions. If a group of people decide you are out—you are an outcast! This could allow you to lose your job and other important life necessities. Fortunately, God is a loving and forgiving Father and is always there waiting to bestow His amazing grace on sinners.

When Jesus walked this earth, the apostle Peter asked Him how many times, he should forgive someone who offended him. "Seven times?" Peter asked. Jesus replied, "No, not seven times, but seventy times seven" (Matthew 18:22 NLT). Jesus then started speaking in parables about people who do not forgive others and yet expect others to forgive them when they mess up. When Jesus taught us how to pray the Our Father Prayer, part of it says, "For if you forgive other people when they sin against you, your Heavenly Father will also forgive you. But if you do not forgive others their sins, your Father will not forgive your sins" (Matthew 6: 14-15 NIV). Just to be clear, this means that people who will not forgive others, will not be forgiven by God when they ask Him for forgiveness. Although it may be hard to live in this judgmental world and even frightening at times, rest assured that if you repent of your sins they will be forgiven by God—if you forgive others for their sins. Jesus died for this very purpose and His blood covers ours sins once we have repented and accepted His gift of salvation.

BATTLE PLAN: God is your defender, and He has promised throughout the ages that He will restore the years that the locust hath eaten (Joel 2:25 KJV). If someone has "canceled" you, God will bring you a better job, better friends, and you will have a place in His society! Choose this day to get rid of your guilt and begin to live again in freedom. If, however, you realize that you have become part of this judgmental culture, you may want to think about where you will be spending eternity. If you decide you would rather spend it in heaven and not hell, ask God for forgiveness, but first you must forgive those who have offended you.

BATTLE SONG: "Mistakes" by Unspoken

FIGHTING FEAR & GAINING GROUND

"You would have no power over me if it were not given you from above." —John 19:11

Whenever I entered my cousin Sissy's house, I would see a beautiful painting of Jesus walking on the water. The story behind this picture is found in Matthew 14:22-33. Jesus had just fed five thousand people and told his disciples to get into their boat and go to the other side of the sea; He was going to stay behind and pray. During the journey the wind suddenly accelerated, and the boat was buffeted by the overpowering ocean. A little before dawn the disciples saw someone walking on the water toward them and they were petrified. Once Jesus spoke and told them not to be afraid, they realized who it was. Peter said, "Lord if it is You, command me to come to You on the water." Jesus replied, "Come" (v. 28-29 NKJ). Some of you know how the story goes; Peter steps out of the boat and starts walking on top of the water toward Jesus, but as soon as Peter looks at his surroundings he begins to sink. Jesus saves him and says, "O you of little faith, why did you doubt" (Matthew 14:31 NKJ). This shows us that if we have faith, we can do unbelievable things.

If I had to pick a person in the Bible that I was most like, it would be Peter. Like Peter, I often speak without thinking and sometimes believe that I can handle more than I really can. I can easily make conjectures and not consider all the consequences. Even though I know that I will encounter opposition from Satan when I am doing something for God's kingdom, I often underestimate the severity of the attacks, because I do not realize the importance of my operation and how many people it will affect. Perhaps you have experienced a time when you underestimated your enemy on the battlefield. It is usually a mistake that you will never forget. However, God still has a plan for your life — maybe He wants to use your warrior skills to help others survive the battle they are in. God knows your worth and so does Satan. As such, the enemy will want to stop your mission before it begins.

It is during these times that the devil hits us with his heaviest artillery, so we must keep our eyes on the Lord. Remember, Peter began to sink only when he looked at the raging sea around him rather than Jesus. When we focus on our circumstances our perception is skewed because our minds are finite. God tells us in His word that "as the heavens are higher than the earth, so are my ways higher than your ways, and my thoughts than your thoughts" (Isaiah 55:9 KJV). Therefore, even though it appears that things are hopeless—they are not! Don't let Satan fill your mind with confusion and unbelief. Trust the King who reigns over heaven and earth.

BATTLE PLAN: Just as God controls the sea, He will determine what his soldiers will endure. As Christians, nothing can touch us unless our Heavenly Father allows it to. Since He created us, He knows our limits better than we do. He has promised that He will never leave or forsake us (Deuteronomy 31:6) and it is through the raging waters that we learn to say, "I can do all things through Christ who gives me strength" (Philippians 4:13 NLT). Is God calling you to step out of your comfort zone, into the tempestuous ocean? I once heard someone say that the safest place to ever be is in the center of God's will. Don't let fear and doubt keep you from getting out of the boat. Step out today and experience all God has for you!

BATTLE SONG: "Walking on Water" by NeedtoBreathe

COMMIT TO THE WAR
& GAIN FREEDOM

"I exhort you also to take part in the great combat, which is the combat of life, and greater than every other conflict." —*Plato*

I think it is safe to say that throughout life, people commit to many things: relationships, credit card payments, mortgages, car loans, and employment responsibilities are a few examples. People in the armed forces also commit to serve for a specific amount of time, as well as pledge an oath to the United States Constitution. In a contract, or as the Bible calls it a covenant, both parties agree to perform certain obligations that require a level of trust for all of those involved. God made many covenants with the people of the Old Testament: never to flood the earth again (Genesis 9:8-11), the blessing to all nations through Abraham (Genesis 12:2), the ten commandments (Exodus 20 KJV), and the dynasty He would build for David (1 Chronicle 17). Because people were unable to keep their part of the commitment, God sent His Son, Jesus, to Earth, which provided a new covenant that we would be able to keep. If we believe in His Son, Jesus, and surrender our lives to Him, we will be forgiven for our sins and spend eternity in heaven. There is a misconception of this agreement that some people have: they believe that when they accept the Lord as their savior, that life will be free of trials. On the contrary, life will become more difficult because our new covenant puts us under grace and on God's side, opposed to being under the law and the sway of Satan. Therefore, the devil will do everything he can to get us back under his command and away from God. In physical wars between nations, some people try to stay neutral, however, the Bible tells us that we must choose to be either hot or cold, we cannot be lukewarm (Revelation 3:15-16).

How are we supposed to fight in a spiritual war? It's one thing to fight against physical enemies that we can see, but how do we engage in combat with someone/something that we can't see? Ephesians 6:10-18 (KJV) tells us to put on *"the whole armor of God"*—truth, righteousness, peace, faith, and prayer. We fight our enemy with "the

185

sword of the Spirit, which is the word of God." Our salvation and commitment to God, allows Him to go before us and assess the enemy's location and weapons of destruction, so He can prepare us for the current battle. The best thing about it is that the Lord will be right by our side fighting with us. We also know the beginning from the end—our side wins! Therefore, let's decide right now, to take part in the combat against the spirits of fear, depression, and hopelessness.

BATTLE PLAN: Despair is something we cannot see, but we can certainly feel, so in order to win the war against it we must use the battle strategies in Ephesians 6. Our enemy is sly; like a spider, he likes to create webs of discouragement and anxiety in our minds. He works day and night building his sticky web that keeps us from moving forward or retreating, so we are stuck in place and at his mercy. The webs that spiders build in our houses can be easily destroyed with the swipe of our hand because the silk they used to spin them is light. It is the web's stickiness that catches the prey. Similarly, God can easily destroy the webs that Satan spins, but we often chose to remain stuck in place. There is no web too sticky that God cannot deliver us out of. Therefore, we must pray and ask God to help us. Once we are free from our captivity, we must always wear our armor so that we do not get captured again. It's important to know everything about our sword (God's word) and to never be without it.

BATTLE SONG: "See A Victory" by Elevation Worship

LOSE ALL THAT HINDERS YOUR PROGRESS

"Can two walk together unless they are agreed?" —*Amos 3:3*

When two or more people are trying to accomplish an objective, they must agree with the execution of their goal. People generally have different opinions on how to approach situations and what strategy is the best method to bring success. Usually, there is someone overseeing the operation, whether it be a parent, a boss, or a superior officer. Without a leader to iron out the differences on the team there would be chaos, so an authoritative figure is important.

Situations become a little more complicated in personal relationships, as there is no leader that decides whether you travel east or west. The pull for control can be exhausting and damaging. However, "a threefold cord is not quickly broken" (Ecclesiastes 4:12 KJV). When God is the center cord in the relationship, He can keep it together, but both people must yield to His guidance.

Since God is so powerful, one would think that He controls our decisions, yet the Bible tells us otherwise. "The Lord is the Spirt, and where the Spirit of the Lord is there is freedom" (2 Corinthians 3:17 NIV). This means that God gives us free will to do whatever we want to in life. I believe that this gift of freedom can be a curse or a blessing. When we make decisions based on our feelings, chase after the newest and best technology, or try to keep up with our neighbors we lead a life that is an emotional rollercoaster. However, when we walk with God and allow Him to guide us, we can have peace knowing that He will be with us no matter what we encounter.

BATTLE PLAN: Surrendering our life to God, does not mean we lose control over our choices; we don't have to go in the direction He wants us to. However, having a loving counselor, protector, and friend walking through the challenging terrain of life with us is a partnership that is irreplaceable. Charles Spurgeon said this about God: "He is the almighty watcher, a sleepless guardian, and a faithful friend." So, why wouldn't we agree to walk with somebody that loves us unconditionally, never sleeps, and knows the plans of our enemy! There was a saying in the 1970s that said, "if you love someone set them free. If they come back, they are yours; if they don't, they never were." God has let us live freely; would He be able say that you are His? If you once were and left Him, it's not too late to run back to Him. If you are His, stay in agreement with His guidance, and you will be on the path that will fulfill your purpose in life.

BATTLE SONG: "Me Without You" by TobyMac

A TIME TO KEEP, AND A TIME TO THROW AWAY
—ECCLESIASTES 3:6B

KEEP ENDURING

"I was given a thorn in my flesh, a messenger of Satan, to torment me. Three times I pleaded with the LORD to take it away from me. But he said to me 'my grace is sufficient for you, for my power is made perfect in weakness.'" —2 Corinthians 12:7-9 (NIV)

Military recruits go through extreme conditions to prove that they will be capable of handling whatever they face during deployment. It could be said that a "thorn in the flesh" is the pain that is afflicted during boot camp, and it is not removed until the instructor determines the limit of pain that can be tolerated. This tactic not only builds endurance for the people in training, but also builds a trust relationship among the team members and their instructor. Similarly, our relationship with the Lord works the same way once we surrender our life to Him.

Yielding to God and His will for our lives requires dedication and complete trust in Him. Sometimes He takes off His hedge of protection around us and lets Satan inflict some pain. The book of Job in the Bible is a perfect example of this. Job lost everything he had: his children, his wealth, all his animals, and even his health. Job did not appear to have committed a crime or sin, and neither did the apostle Paul (referenced in the opening scripture). So, one would wonder why God would allow the enemy to hurt his people.

According to the Bible, Satan approached God and said that Job was only loyal to Him because God had blessed him mightily. So, God took His hedge of protection off of Job, but would not let Satan lay a hand on him (Job 1:1-12). Job passed the test and stayed loyal to God, and God blessed him with more than he had before he was afflicted. Paul, however, was told by God, "My grace is sufficient for you, for My strength is made perfect in weakness." Paul accepted the Lord's answer and went on to do amazing things for God's kingdom, even with his infirmity.

These stories in the Bible show us that there are no set rules for God's behavior. Job's health was restored and so was everything he lost, but Paul had to live with his pain. However, both accounts illustrate that God gave Job and Paul the strength they needed to persevere. It also showed the people around them that their strength had to come from God because no human could endure the things that they did. It is the testimonies of people in the past and those living around us that give us hope and encouragement to continue on the journey.

BATTLE PLAN: The enemy loves to see us injured or weak because he knows that we are more likely to give up if more pain is afflicted. Sometimes, even the threat of more pain is enough for us to raise the white flag. Therefore, we must remember that God is in control and Satan is limited to what he can do to God's children. If, however, we have walked away from God and His protection, we may be open game to the enemy; if that's the case, it would be wise to run back to God immediately. It is so important for us to stay close to Him especially when we are weak. We need to ask God to strengthen/heal us and give us guidance on how to proceed. He is our commander and chief and He knows our limitations. What He allows to affect us will make us stronger and build our endurance. We can block the enemies' threats and attacks by reading the Bible, praying, and worshipping. When we are overwhelmed, we need to reach out to one of our friends or family members to help us in the battle. They can pray for us and encourage us when we are too weak to do it ourselves. Remember God's faithfulness thus far and stay strong!

BATTLE SONG: "Out of My Hands" by Jeremy Camp

KEEP FIGHTING

"I have not yet begun to fight." —*John Paul Jones*

American Naval Captain John Paul Jones made the above comment when he was asked to surrender his ship. His tenacity and will to win was admirable and he was determined to keep his ship. People fight for many reasons: sometimes they fight for freedom, sometimes for protection, and sometimes for justice.

There is an old saying: "The squeaky wheel gets the oil," meaning that the noise will bring attention to a need and eventually it will get fixed because the sound is annoying. Jesus shared a story with His disciples about a widow who approached a judge regarding a dispute she had with her enemy. The judge kept ignoring her demands, but her persistence finally got to him. He said, "this woman is driving me crazy. I'm going to see that she gets justice because she is wearing me out with her constant requests!" Jesus shared this parable (Luke 18:5 NLT) with His disciples to make the point that we should never give up asking God for things, even if it appears that He is ignoring us. Of course, what we ask for must be something that lines up with His word; we can't ask Him for someone else's spouse or for money to commit sin. In the case of the widow, she was looking for the "oil" of justice, which by law she was biblically entitled to.

Charles Spurgeon once said, "In the way the sun never grows weary of shining, nor a stream of flowing, it is God's nature to keep His promises. Therefore, go immediately to His throne and say, 'Do as You promised.'" We don't know why God is not fulfilling our requests, but regardless of the reason, we must never give up petitioning Him.

BATTLE STRATEGY: We must have the tenacity the widow in the parable had and keep asking God for what we need; remember, most battles are won on our knees. We must have the tenacity John Paul Jones had, and let the enemy know that we are going to fight even harder to overcome his attacks. Satan wants us to believe that God isn't answering our prayers because He doesn't care about us or our situation. If the devil can't get us mad at God, he will try to convince us to take matters into our own hands. We mustn't fall for this trap, but rather keep persevering and having faith that God will fulfill our needs. As we trust in His timing, we will discover that it is always perfect!

BATTLE SONG: "Fight on Fighter" by for King and Country

KEEP PERSEVERING

"Patience and perseverance have a magical effect before which difficulties and obstacles vanish." —*John Quincy Adams*

Sports have been around for thousands of years. All different cultures and civilizations found excitement and joy watching and rooting for their favorite athlete or team. The Romans had their chariot races and Ancient Greece had their Olympic games dating back to 776 BC. I was raised by parents who loved watching sports—hockey football, baseball, golf, or the Olympics. During the game/competition our minds were free from the worries of life. There is something about seeing your favorite athlete achieve success by beating the odds or breaking records that brings a smile to your face and a feeling victory. We also feel happy for their success because we know the amount of perseverance and training it took to get them there.

During the COVID lockdowns sports were canceled and people were in isolation. Many people could not see their family members and it was very hard for the people who lived alone; those people more than ever needed to watch something uplifting and encouraging because the news was depressing and frightening to many. Once sports were able to reconvene, fans were not allowed to be in the stands. Although they were excited to watch their teams play, many of the players felt that competing wasn't the same because the fans were not present to cheer them on. This clearly showed that people need to interact with one another and have something that they find joy in; it also showed the importance of us cheering each other on to victory.

People learned a lot about themselves during COVID. Some people were productive and worked on projects that they never had time for in the past, while others, unfortunately, turned to alcohol or drugs. Many turned to God because they were afraid or realized that what is described as the end times in the Bible might be happening. Those of us who already had a relationship with the Lord, found peace and encouragement as we sought His word daily. When the hardships of life are overwhelming and there is nobody there to comfort and inspire us, we must remember that Jesus said, "I am with you always, even unto the end of the world" (Matthew 28:20 KJV). In addition to that we are "surrounded by such a great crowd of witnesses, let us throw off everything that hinders and the sin that so easily entangles, and let us run with perseverance the race marked out for us, fixing our eyes on Jesus, the pioneer and perfecter of our faith. For the joy set before him he endured the cross, scorning its shame, and sat down at the right hand of the throne of God" (Hebrews 12:1-2 NIV). Charles Spurgeon once said, "By perseverance the snail reached the ark." It doesn't matter how fast we get to our destination, but that we DO get there eventually. When we are by ourselves and we have nobody to encourage us, listening to worship music and reading God's word can give us the boost we need to keep persevering.

BATTLE PLAN: Sports and Olympic team members have competitors who want to triumph over them. All the athletes have trained well, but only one person, or one team will win the prize. Satan, your fieriest competitor, knows that God allows everyone to win the prize of salvation, if they accept the gift that is offered through His Son's death. When our opponent is overpowering us, we must remember that God has and will equip us with everything we need to win the race because we are on His team!

BATTLE SONG: "The Victory" by Third Day

KEEPING OUR EYES ON JESUS

"There is nothing in a caterpillar that tells you it's going to be a butterfly." —R. *Buckminster Fuller*

Many people think that once they accept Christ as their Lord and Savior their life will be easier. On the contrary—it usually gets harder if we are truly all in for Him. Just like someone who enlists in the armed forces surrenders most of their freedoms, Christians commit to give up their sinful ways and yield control of their life to God's command. Once they do, boot camp begins, and God allows situations to occur that will push their limits and cause fatigue. This training develops their trust in their leader's ability to lead, but also in their own ability to endure. As soldiers, they hear stories and witness events of those who have gone before them, proving that suffering, resilience, and perseverance are part of the equation that leads to victory.

Some warriors have given the ultimate sacrifice—death—to further the cause they believe in, while others survive the battle, but the war still rages on in their minds. General Douglas MacArthur once said, "The soldier above all others prays for peace, for it is the soldier who must suffer and bear the deepest wounds and scars of war." When Jesus resurrected after His crucifixion, His scars were the visible signs of the victory He won, and a reminder of the price He paid for us. It is the scars we incur in life that remind us of our past victories and keep us in the battle.

Some of the missions that God sets before us look scary and challenging. They may consist of cancer, the death of a loved one, or financial loss. It is when we are at our weakest state that the enemy attacks the hardest. We are told in Ephesians 6:12 (NLT) that "we are not fighting against flesh and blood enemies, but against evil rulers and authorities of the unseen word." The enemy will fire rockets of lies saying that your commander has abandoned you and you are on your own. During this time, Satan will try to cut off any communications that you can have with God and others who will support and encourage you. Therefore, it is paramount to keep your eyes fixed on Jesus and His ability to see you through the battle; He has fought the fight and won. He knows exactly what you need and will provide you with it—trust in Him!

BATTLE STRATEGY: When we start boot camp as a soldier for God, we are caterpillars; however, God see us as the butterfly we can become. Caterpillars actually devour themselves during the metamorphosis process. In Christianity, this process is called "dying to self." God created the caterpillar to have everything it needs for the changeover, and He will provide everything we need as well. Satan wants us to think that we will never amount to anything, and that we are done growing. God is rooting for us to believe in the transformation He can do in our lives. We can choose to not conform and crawl through life or go through the turmoil that it takes to become butterflies and fly like God wants us to.

BATTLE SONG: "Changed" by Jordan Feliz

Throwing Away Your Insecurities

"Our bodies have many parts and God has put each part just where he wants it."
—1 Corinthians 12:18 (NLT)

The human body's structure has systems that depend on each other to function.

The circulatory system contains the heart that pumps blood through our body and carries oxygen to our cells. The respiratory system houses the lungs, breathes in oxygen, and expels the carbon dioxide within us. The integumentary system includes the skin that keeps out bacteria and disease. The skeletal system consists of bones, ligaments, and cartilage that protects our organs; the marrow in the long bones constructs immune cells. Our muscular system has various types of muscles that allow us to move. The digestive system processes our food that keeps our cells alive. The environment inside our body is regulated by the endocrine system that releases hormones that are vital to the body's function. The excretory system holds the kidneys that keep our blood clean. When anything foreign enters our body, it is the lymphatic system that reproduces cells that attack it. Whereas our reproductive system provides cells that allow us to produce offspring. All these systems must work together to keep a person healthy.

God designed each system in the human body to have its own purpose. However, each system and each body part within that system, work together for the good of the body as a whole. "If the foot says, 'I am not a part of the body because I am not a hand,' that does not make it any less a part of the body. And if the ear says, 'I am not part of the body because I am not an eye," would that make it any less a part of the body? If the whole body were an eye, how would you hear? Or if your whole body were an ear, how would you smell anything?... The eye can never say to the hand, 'I don't need you?' The head can't say to the feet, "I don't need you." (1 Corinthians 12:15-16, 21 NLT). In fact, some parts of the body that seem weakest and least important are actually the most necessary. Similarly, people need each other because all of us have certain characteristics that are unique that we can contribute to society. God specifically placed our talents and gifts inside of us, so that we could combine them with other people's gifts to make a difference in the world and also in God's kingdom. Therefore, don't believe the enemy's voice whispering in your head that you are useless, you do not have what it takes—because you do!

BATTLE PLAN: "God chose the foolish things of the world to shame the wise; God chose the weak things of the world to shame the strong. God chose the lowly things of this world and the despised things—and the things that are not—to nullify the things that are, so that no one may boast before him" (1 Corinthians 1:27-29 NIV). Some examples of this scripture in action were David, a young shepherd boy who took down the giant Goliath with a sling and a stone; Esther, a Jewish girl, who became queen of Persia and saved the Jewish nation from annihilation; and Joseph, a slave, who became the second most powerful man in Egypt. When God partners with us to complete a mission, nothing can prevent it from happening, except for our unwillingness to participate! God gives us freewill, so He will not force us to be part of His team. However, He often allows trials in our lives that push us toward His path for us. Don't ever think that you have nothing to contribute; God's plan has a part that only you can fulfill, and He believes in you! When we focus on what we can do and not what we can't do, God is able to use us in ways we never could have imagined.

BATTLE SONG: "He Believes in You" by Danny Gokey

THROWING AWAY YOUR COINS OF DOUBT

"If anyone thirsts, let him come to Me and drink. He who believes in Me, as the Scripture has said, out of his heart will flow rivers of living water." —John 7:37-38 (NKJ)

There are fountains throughout the world, and some are more famous than others. I have had the pleasure of visiting the Trevi Fountain in Rome on two different occasions. Rumor has it that if you throw a coin into the fountain, it will guarantee a return trip to the city; a second coin ensures romance; a third coin leads to marriage. The history behind the fountain tells us that the water was originally used for drinking and came from an aqueduct. Today, the same water is recirculated from the pool and up through the heart of the fountain and out.

In 2007, I went to Mexico on a mission trip. I did not know how to speak Spanish, but I knew that God wanted to use me as a vessel to pour out His love on the children there. I prayed that His love would flow out of me, and it did, especially for one two-year-old boy named Juan Jose. He and his brother, Miguel, lived at an orphanage with fifty other children. Their parents brought them there because they could not afford to take care of them. The government would not allow the children at this orphanage to be adopted. Therefore, the kids would live at the orphanage until they were adults, unless their parents decided to them out of the orphanage. Just like a fountain needs water to flow through it to create a soothing sound that brings tranquility, a child needs the reassuring love of someone to know that everything will be okay. On my first day at the orphanage, Juan Jose was walking around crying; I picked him up and held him until he fell asleep. The next day, he looked for me and he was by my side the whole day. On our last day at the orphanage, I was holding Juan Jose as he slept. One of the girls on our trip did not engage with the children but helped the woman who ran the orphanage by doing chores. She said to the lady, *"I do not know how to speak Spanish, so I can't interact with the kids."* The lady replied, *"There is no language barrier when it comes to love*" and pointed to me. Jesus says, "You do not have because you do not ask God" (James 4:2 NIV). The difference between me and my teammate was that I was not depending on my own ability, and I prayed for God to fill me with His love for the children. When we ask God for help, we become the coins that bring blessings to others. Once we experience God's living waters flowing through our hearts and out, we will never thirst again.

The money that is thrown into the Trevi Fountain is collected every day and averages about 3,000 euro per day. This money is used to buy food for the poor and homeless. I imagine that people who throw their coins into the fountain to make a wish have no idea that they are making an impact on the life of someone who is struggling. I have no idea if my time spent with Juan Jose impacted his life, but it certainly impacted mine!

BATTLE STRATEGY: Mohandas Gandhi said, "The best way to find yourself, is to lose yourself in the service of others." Everyone is born with unique gifts to contribute to society. If you find yourself not engaging in life, perhaps your pool is empty and there is no water available to flow out of you. If so, it is time to *ask God* to fill your heart today with His living waters, so that you don't miss out on the healing He has for you and the new season He wants you to begin. As the healing water is recycled through your body, your coins of doubt, insecurity, and depression can be changed into faith, trust, and hope. Then God can use you as a reservoir for people who are looking for a place to throw their coins of despair and hopelessness.

BATTLE SONG: "All Who Are Thirsty" by Kutless

KEEP MOVING

"Moses told the people, 'Don't be afraid. Just stand where you are and watch the Lord rescue you…. The Lord himself will fight for you. Just stay calm.' Then the Lord said to Moses, 'Why are your crying out to me? Tell the people to get moving. Pick up your staff and raise your hand over the sea. Divide the water so the Israelites can walk through the middle of the sea on dry ground.'" —Exodus 14:13-16 (NLT)

When we are fighting to survive, there are many scenarios that can occur. At times we need to wait, other times we retreat, and sometimes we advance. In the opening scripture, the Israelites were fleeing from Egypt and were trapped; the red sea was in front of them, and the Egyptians were closing in on them from the rear. It was obvious that if the people did nothing, Pharaoh's army would capture or kill them.

God told Moses to take the Israelites to the promise land; so, when Moses cried out to Him, He told Moses how to proceed. Moses did what the Lord said, and they escaped death, and Pharaoh's army drowned in the sea. There are stories like this throughout the Bible, but do we believe them? Perhaps you have encountered a situation that you know it was God who kept you alive. I know that God has saved me multiple times while on the mission field.

In the fall of 2010, I went on a mission trip to Jacmel, Haiti. The country was still recovering from an earthquake; there were a million people living in tents the week we arrived, and a cholera outbreak was spreading through the tent population. I was a surgical technologist at the time and one of my teammates was a pediatrician, but we were not allowed to treat patients because we did not get clearance from the Haitian government before we arrived. So, instead we volunteered at an orphanage in the area and helped the community prepare for a Category 3 hurricane that was predicted to hit during the week. We were told that the Mission Aviation Fellowship (MAF) planes would not be able to fly over the mountains to get us and bring us to Port-au-Prince, so we made calls to our families and told them that we could lose electricity for a long time and would contact them whenever we could. I told my daughter to have our church pray that

God would reroute the hurricane or at least downgrade it. The mission house we were staying in would not be safe during the storm, so we were prepared to move to another location. We got a call the next day saying that two MAF planes would land in Jacmel and fly us to Port-au-Prince. We got the last flight out of Haiti. It was filled with other missionaries, and it was the quietest flight I have ever been on; we were all praying for the people. God answered our prayers, the Category 3 hurricane was downgraded to a Category 1 when it hit Haiti. We obeyed God's orders to move, and the Haitians saw the Lord rescue them.

BATTLE PLAN: C. S. Lewis said, "Getting over a painful experience is much like crossing the monkey bars. You have to let go at some point in order to move forward." The Israelites were slaves in Egypt for years. God wanted them to enter the promised land, but the journey was scary. When the Red Sea was parted, they had to walk on the ocean floor not knowing if the walls of water would cave in; they trusted God, made it through, and God destroyed their enemy. What steps is God calling us to take to free us from the captivity of fear or depression? Our enemy is going to keep coming after us, just like Pharaoh's army pursued the Israelites. However, if we let go of one monkey bar in faith to grasp another, God can move us on to victory. He wants us to fight our enemy and He will provide cover fire for us, but we must move on in order to secure the victory.

BATTLE SONG: "Egypt" by Cory Asbury

KEEPING THE FAITH

"We walk by faith not by sight." —2 Corinthians 5:7

During a snowstorm or hurricane, we often lose electricity. Sometimes when this occurs, we happen to be away from the lantern or the flashlight that we left in another room. If we are in our own home, we are able to find our way in the darkness to that room. Knowing the layout of the house well enables us to avoid things in the dark that could cause us to stumble. Nevertheless, we would still walk cautiously through each room. If we happened to have a house guest during that time, we would also lead them to a safe place to sit—if, of course, they were willing to trust our guidance. Hopefully, they would follow our lead knowing that we would be the one to fall over any obstacle in the way because we were walking in front of them. If they did not trust us, they would have to stay in the dark where they were until the electricity was restored or until the sun rose in the morning. Can you see the comparison of God trying to lead us in the dark?

God knows all about the darkness because He created it (Genesis 1:2-5) and has a purpose for it. As such, He would be the best one to lead us out of it and into the light. Why then, do we hesitate to ask God to guide us? Is it pride, unbelief, or is it because we do not know Him? The last reason is a poor excuse because when we are lost, we usually have no problem asking a stranger for directions. However, some of us would rather trust the North Star in the dark of night because we know when we are facing it, we will be heading north. This does allow us to get our bearings, but we have no idea what dangers are lurking in that direction. So, why not ask the one who named and placed the North Star in the sky? We put our faith in stars, people, and compasses because we can see them, however, true faith is when we put it in the things not seen.

Before the apostle Paul made the statement above in 2 Corinthians 5:7, he was telling the people of Corinth that things that are seen in this world are temporary, and we should not focus on them because they are not eternal. The trials and sufferings in life are only for a short time compared to the joy and peace we will experience for eternity in heaven. Hebrews 11:1 says, "Faith is the substance of things hoped for, the evidence of things not seen." Chapter 11 in the book of Hebrews talks about all the amazing things that people like Noah and Abraham accomplished because they followed God's guidance, even when people thought they were crazy. Their minds were focused on God's will and eternity, not on what they were seeing.

BATTLE PLAN: When we find ourselves in the darkness of despair and cannot see the light at the end of the tunnel, we have a choice to make. We can sit in the dark and hope that we will survive the night, or we can ask God to guide us through the darkness. As we put our faith in Him, He walks before us and deals with all the obstacles in our path so that we can accomplish His purpose for our lives. Each time we walk by faith and not sight during our journey in this world, we build trust in God's guidance and obtain a peace that surpasses all understanding (Philippians 4:7). This change in us, not only saves us from a life of anxiety, but it lights the path for others in the dark to follow.

BATTLE SONG: "That's What Faith Can Do" by Kutless

Throw Away Your Agenda

"His pleasure is not in the strength of the horse, nor his delight in the legs of the warrior, the LORD delights in those who fear him, who put their hope in his unfailing love." —Psalm 147:10-11 (NIV)

Racehorses are beautiful animals. They have physical strength, as well as endurance. In the wild, they run with the wind on open plains. On racetracks., they run with the best of the best. They are trained and conditioned to win, and to keep persevering until they reach the finish line. If they come in first place, they are crowned with a wreath of flowers. As these prizewinners age and can no longer perform to the standards required, they are "put out to pasture." God, however, created these purebreds to have multiple purposes, just like he did with human beings.

Did you know that horses have the ability to sense people's emotions and will react to them? If somebody on a horse is afraid, the steed will try to figure out what is near them that is causing the person to fear. The medical profession has used these intuitive animals for years to help humans overcome trauma and depression, or simply to build up their confidence. Even though some of our equestrian friends had a season in their life where they were praised by men as being great champions that broke records, I believe that God finds joy in the "out to pasture" season of the racehorse's life. It is there that the horse makes its greatest contribution—helping individuals overcome the obstacles that hinder them from moving forward.

People also have an "out to pasture" season in their life as well—it is called retirement. When one envisions this stage of life in their mind, they may think of the elderly generation, however, sometimes it is an illness or disability that allows the change of the season to come early. It often arrives when someone is finally achieving their goals, or when a mighty warrior is making great strides on the battlefield. It's during these times that we need to remember that God has a purpose in everything He allows to happen. Just like the racehorse, He may want to use our gifts to help others. The above scripture states that God does not take great pleasure in our strength, but rather in the reverence people have for Him. The "fear" listed in

Psalm 147:10-11 is the kind that a person would have for their boss or superior officer—a respect and confidence in their leadership.

"Some trust in chariots and some in horses: but we will remember the name of the Lord our God" (Psalm 20:7 KJV). God gave me that scripture when my life abruptly changed, and I found myself living in a volatile environment. My life's purpose was redirected, I was on unchartered territory, and I chose to put my trust solely in my heavenly Father's hands. He not only helped me with the adjustment, but He showed me characteristics that I never knew I had inside me. My days of running my own race were over; it was time for me to encourage and help others move forward on their journey. Where are you in the race of life?

BATTLE PLAN: God is loving and merciful and it hurts Him to see His children suffer. If your life has been unexpectedly turned upside down, please know that a new season is on the horizon that will allow you to grow in ways that you would not have imagined. What seems so devasting may be the new trail to the best part of your life. Be open to what or who God sends your way to help you—it could be an animal or a person! Once you have been helped, you will find so much joy and fulfillment in paying it forward.

BATTLE SONG: "Future" by Jordan Feliz.

A TIME TO TEAR, AND A TIME TO SEW —ECCLESIASTES 3:7A

TEARING DOWN FALSE IMAGES

"You can identify them by their fruit, that is, by the way they act. Can you pick grapes from thornbushes or figs from thistles? A good tree produces good fruit, and a bad tree produces bad fruit." —Matthew 7:16-17 (NLT)

oes our outward appearance present a true picture of who we really are on the inside? People can often disguise who they are, however, the things of nature cannot. God made animals to be what they are for a specific purpose. My daughter has two dogs: one is sweet and nonconfrontational, and the other one is an alpha dog. As the alpha, he is the pack leader that needs to be aware of everything going on, and he makes us laugh when he is in his "policing mode." He hates it when people move quickly or raise their voices; he barks and tries to get their attention and will even try to herd them into stopping certain actions. The fact that he was rescued from a shelter may contribute to his persistence and resilience as well. When he is relaxing, he sits on top of the back of the couch, which illustrates his hierarchy because he is up higher than everyone. As much as we try to get him to be more laid back, his natural instincts always come out.

I believe that nature works so perfectly because trees, animals, and the weather can only contribute the attributes that were inbred in them. Similarly, people were created with unique characteristics to accomplish specific tasks that contribute to the good of humanity and God's kingdom. However, there is a satanic presence in society that promotes self-importance and perfection; marketing strategies entice us to believe that certain products will make us look younger and certain pills will make us happier, for example. Satan's goal is to take our focus off our purpose in life and put it on ourselves. Our new goal will be to fit into "society," whereas God wants us to "come out from them and be separate" (2 Corinthians 6:17 NIV). With all the hypocrisy and deception in the world today, how can we tell if someone is really who they appear to be? Jesus tells us to look at what a person's labor has produced. Anyone can talk the talk, but the proof is in how they walk their walk. If we find ourselves depressed and not engaging in life, we need to ask ourselves, *"are we trying to please people or God?"* When we are being who were created to be we will have peace and joy, because like animals and nature, we are doing what we were created to do.

BATTLE PLAN: Not all people who are masking their identity have evil or selfish intentions. Perhaps they're masking their identity because they are insecure and feel that people won't like the "real them." Therefore, they cannot produce the "good fruit" they were created to bring into the world. If we are hiding behind a wall of insecurity or vanity, we must tear it down! God's word says that our "beauty should not come from outward adornment… rather, it should be that of your inner self" (1 Peter 3:3,4 NIV). When we find ourselves in a season where there is no growth in our life, it might be because God is pruning us to produce bigger and better fruit in the future. C.S. Lewis said, "There are far, far better things ahead than any we leave behind." It is never too late to change. If we stop striving to "fit in" and remain true to ourselves, we allow God to yield a bountiful crop through our lives that cannot only bless us, but more importantly bless others!

BATTLE SONG: "The Well" by Casting Crowns

TEARING TISSUE & BUILDING MUSCLES

"All things are difficult before they are easy." —*Thomas Fuller*

Anyone who has ever joined a gym and began an exercise program, knows that it is necessary to start small and gradually increase the weight/resistance needed to strengthen and build muscles. In addition to that, people need to rest the muscles that were challenged for at least a day, if not more. This allows the tissues that were damaged to replenish and the glycogen, which breaks down to glucose, to provide energy. If we don't rest, we cause more damage that prevents the muscles from getting stronger. Rest not only replenishes what was depleted, it allows the muscle tissue that was worked to grow back stronger.

Faith works the same way; God allows trials in our lives that put stress and tension on our belief system, so that it will become stronger. Each trial allows our faith to grow, and we are able to endure more pressure and stress. It is extremely important that we rest in the Lord daily so that He can replenish the tears in our faith. If we don't, our faith can become totally depleted. As we seek God's word, He encourages us and we grow spiritually stronger. Each challenge we face builds our muscles of faith and trust.

BATTLE PLAN: The enemy of our soul wants us to be weak and fearful. He will do everything he can to prevent us from reading God's word. Clergyman and historian Thomas Fuller also said, "A book that is shut is but a block." In order to grow our faith, we must participate in the process; after all, our physical muscles are not going to get stronger if we do nothing. Therefore, it us up to us to decide if we want to grow spiritually strong, so that we can fight the enemies' attacks. God knows how much pressure we can endure and He will give us what we need, but we must ask and seek Him. Why is it so easy for us to believe and trust a personal trainer at the gym, but not our heavenly Father who created us? It's easy because Satan is always at work messing with our minds, trying to convince us that God is giving us more than we can handle. The only time this lie becomes true, is if we don't do our part of the workout and rest in the Lord and read His word, so He can build us up!

BATTLE SONG: "Strong Enough" by Matthew West

Tearing Up Our Road Map

"A person's steps are directed by the LORD. How then can anyone understand their own way?"—Proverbs 20:24 (NIV)

It is easy to look back in hindsight and see the wrong choices we made during our life. Some of us live with regrets and can't let go of the past, while others learn from their mistakes and move on. God actually understands the choices we made better than we do because He knows our thoughts, our strengths, and our weaknesses.

If we were to consider the events of our life as puzzle pieces that form the completed puzzle of our life, we would all start out our puzzle in a similar way. As babies we viewed the world as confusing, most of us could hear our parents speak, but we weren't capable of understanding what the words meant, or how to speak back. We witnessed people walking from one place to another, yet we couldn't understand how they got their legs and feet to coordinate movement. As we got a little older and tried to walk, it was like trying to fit a puzzle piece in a spot it wasn't made for. However, as our muscular skeletal system and brain developed, we were able to piece together the components necessary to successfully walk.

As we aged, we became more independent and often tried to force things to fit together instead of waiting for them to happen the way they were supposed to happen. Pieces of relationships, jobs, or investments weren't right for us, yet we wanted them to happen. When they didn't, we often felt discouraged or depressed and maybe cynical, thinking that life and/or God was cruel. When in reality that person, that position, or that investment could have led us down a path that was not good for us. We must remember that from our standpoint, we can only see a section of the puzzle of our life whereas God sees the completed puzzle and knows exactly where each piece belongs to complete the life we were created to have. If we find our lives in pieces right now and we don't know how to put it back together again, we don't have to worry. God knows just how we can reconstruct everything—He is just waiting for us to ask for His guidance.

BATTLE PLAN: There are many strategies to complete a puzzle. Some people empty the box and put all the pieces of the same colors together. Others may look for all the edge pieces and begin with those to construct the border of the puzzle. Yet, other people may study the picture of the puzzle on the box to develop a construction plan. Unfortunately, we don't have access to a picture of our completed life, so we often just sort out the pros and cons of a situation to solve that section of our life and hope for the best. God never intended for us to walk this world alone struggling to figure out the pattern that was designed for our life. Therefore, He does the best He can to direct our steps to complete our life puzzle. It is us who prevent Him from being successful. Evangelist George Mueller once said, "God not only orders our steps, He also orders our stops." When we realize this there is no need for us to despair when our plans don't work out, as long as we are seeking and trusting God to help us complete our life puzzle.

BATTLE SONG: "Your Promises" by Elevation Worship

WEAVING STRENGTH AS WE WAIT

"The disappointments in our lives are really His appointment. They are carefully threaded pieces of yarn in the fabric of our lives that bind the intricate patterns together. They are meant to bring strength and resolve and are not meant to make us frayed." —Alex Adamopoulos

Mistakes are often a part of innovation. Thomas Edison only had about three months of formal education in his entire life, yet he was a genius who invented many things. However, his attempts to create the light bulb were unsuccessful time and time again. When a reporter asked him what it felt like to fail so many times, Edison said, "The light bulb was an invention with a thousand steps." He looked at each failure as a step in the right direction toward success! If we could only have that attitude, life would be less stressful.

How many times do we try something before we give up? The tenacity that Edison had is not seen much in the world today— technology has washed it away. We are so used to having instant answers to our questions online and being able to purchase what we want with a push of a button that we, as a society, have grown impatient.

Sometimes God gives us a vision and we become frustrated because nothing materializes. The prophet Habakkuk in the Old Testament of the Bible was told by God: "Write the vision and make it plain on tablets, that he may run who reads it. For the vision is yet for an appointed time; but at the end it will speak and it will not lie. Though it tarries wait for it; because it will surely come" (Habakkuk 2:2-3 NKJ). The prophet Habakkuk had been crying out to God because evil was prevalent in the world, and he was discouraged. When David in the Bible was on the run from his enemies he cried out to the Lord and then encouraged himself by thinking of God's faithfulness. David said in Psalm 27:13-14 (NKJ), "I would have lost heart, unless I had believed that I would see the goodness of the Lord in the land of the living. Wait on the Lord; be of good courage, and He shall strengthen your heart." God always has a purpose in delaying His answers to our prayers. Habakkuk's prayers were delayed because God was waiting for the people to repent and turn back to Him. David was on the run from his enemies because God was preparing him to be king. It was during David's hardest times that he learned to trust God. What scenario do we find ourselves in today? Whichever one it is, we can be confident that God will finish what He began in us. While we wait, we need to be optimistic like Edison and ask God to strengthen us.

BATTLEPLAN: When we find ourselves discouraged like Habakkuk was because of the evil in the world; hiding from people who are trying to harm us like David; or working to create the vision we saw like Edison was, we must remember that God is in control and His timing is always perfect. "Since ancient times no one has heard, no ear has perceived, no eye has seen any God besides you, who acts on behalf of those who wait for him" (Isaiah 64:4 NIV). While we wait for God to work in our situation, He will be threading the delicate pieces of frayed disappointments together, that will strengthen us to accomplish our mission!

BATTLE SONG: "I Have This Hope" by Tenth Avenue North

SEWING A NEW WARDROBE

"Eat to please thyself, but dress to please others." —Benjamin Franklin

Benjamin Franklin died in 1790. Although times were different back then, somethings never change. According to Franklin, we should dress to earn favor with people. Today, this phrase has been updated to "dress for success." While the world looks at the outward appearance of a person, God is concerned with their heart (1 Samuel 16:7 KJV). We know this is true because when King Saul of Israel was being replaced, the prophet Samuel was looking at men's physical size and appearance, so that the new king would be comparable to Saul. God rejected the men that Samuel thought were fit to reign and instructed him to anoint David, a shepherd boy, who was definitely not dressed for success, even according to the standards of those days.

The world today is much different; technology has made it easy for people to pretend to be someone that they are not. Plus, it is hard for people to fit into certain societies or even be noticed if they do not wear the newest stye of clothing or expensive shoes/sneakers. Fortunately, we do not have to worry about our outward appearance with God—He loves us for who are, not for what we have or what we wear. When Jesus walked this earth, He wore a simple tunic that was made with one piece of material, rather than two (John 19:23 KJV). Author Mark Twain once said, "Be careless in your dress if you must, but keep a tidy soul." Twain understood what was important. Jesus said, "So, why do you worry about clothing? Consider the lilies of the field, how they grow: they neither toil nor spin; and yet I say to you that even Solomon in all his glory was not arrayed like one of these. Now if God so clothes the grass of the field, which today is, and tomorrow is thrown into the oven, will He not much more clothe you, O you of little faith (Matthew 6:28-30 NKJ)? If we follow God's ways, He will elevate our status at work and in society if that is part of His plan for our life. Therefore, instead of trying to impress and please people, we need to sew a new wardrobe, one that honors and pleases God.

God gives us instructions on what our clothes should consist of in Colossians 3:12 (NIV): "As God's chosen people, holy and dearly loved, clothe yourselves with compassion, kindness, humility, gentleness, and patience." When we make these alterations to our wardrobe, we will be dressed for success in God's eyes. We may also stand out in a crowd of people as well. Either way, we will be ready for God to elevate us and move us closer to our destiny.

BATTLE PLAN: The enemy wants us to believe that in order to be popular, respected, and happy we need to fit into the world's pattern for success. Remember, Satan is the father of lies and knows that what society offers will never fulfill our lives—only God can. When our heavenly Father created us, He stitched unique gifts and talents inside each one of us, making us perfectly tailored for our purpose and our relationships. Remember, we are not called to fit in, and we have all we need for success because we are clothed in the righteousness of Christ.

BATTLE SONG: "Resurrection Power" by Chris Tomlin

CREATING A PATTERN FOR HAPPINESS

"The happiness of your life depends upon the quality of your thoughts: therefore, guard accordingly." —Marcus Aurelius

The world has its standards of success and failure, good and bad. Some people make decisions on what society is currently defining as "successful" or "good." The problem with letting others create these standards is that people are led by their emotions—as such, their beliefs can be swayed. C. S. Lewis put it this way, "Don't let your happiness depend on something you may lose." This saying covers many things that society states will lead to joy: the perfect spouse, your dream home, your own business, and of course hitting megabucks. Purchasing our dream house is so exciting until the novelty wears off and we are sick of spending our weekend cleaning the enormous house and mowing the grass. When things go wrong with our new business and we are stressed trying to keep it open, our marriage often struggles as well. Hitting the lottery is usually a temporary fix because managing the money, paying the taxes, and not knowing if people like us for us or our money becomes an issue. All these things consume our thoughts, which most likely leads to worry, anxiety, and fear of possibly losing everything, which makes us extremely unhappy.

When Jesus walked this earth He told his disciples, "It is easier for a camel to go through the eye of a needle than for a rich man to enter into the kingdom of God" (Matthew 19:24 KJV). This is quite a statement; I find it difficult to even get a piece of fine thread through a needle so I can sew something. During the days of Jesus and up to a few decades ago, many people made their own clothes, or at least sewed together the tears in their shirts and pants, or darned socks. They valued the amount of time and effort that went into making the clothes. Nowadays, people can throw out the ripped clothing and purchase new items easily, so clothes are not valued very much.

Marcus Aurelius said that our happiness depends on our thought process, which we should "guard accordingly." So, what does that mean? The apostle Paul learned the secret of perseverance and peace through his suffering and developed this pattern for happiness: "be anxious for nothing, but in everything by prayer and supplication, with thanksgiving let your request be made known to God. And the peace of God, which surpasses all understanding, will guard your hearts and minds through Christ Jesus" (Philippians 4:6-7 NKJ). When we let go of worldly things and yield to the Lord's plans for our life, we will find happiness. I know this to be true because He created us with a specific purpose in mind for our lives. When we are using the gifts that He threaded into our personalities to accomplish the vision, we will be our happiest!

BATTLE PLAN: Andre Gide, who is an author and Nobel Prize winner said, "It is easier to lead men to combat, than direct them toward the patient labors of peace." We are so used to our minds being in a state of conflict and confusion that it's hard to center our thoughts on peace and have clarity. Changing our thought process can be difficult, but we don't have to do it alone. The Bible tells us to "Let the Spirit renew your thoughts and attitudes" (Ephesians 4:23 NLT). When we surrender to God and ask for help, we are on our way to creating a new pattern for happiness. Satan is going to come at us with full force; we must be ready for the attacks. We can't fight this battle on our own, so we must seek God's word and pray for guidance—He will transform us!

BATTLE SONG: "Different" by Micah Tyler

Tearing Down the World's
Influence on Us

"One reason why birds and horses are not unhappy is because they are not trying to impress other birds and horses." —*Salvador Dali*

The world's view of what happiness has changed dramatically over the last few years. Social media has contributed greatly to the change; people are constantly posting things on it about the good things in their life, but not usually the bad. This can be depressing to someone who is currently in a season of their life where everything is going wrong. Some people even use beauty filters to edit their pictures so they look more attractive or younger, which can also make people feel worse. I have heard horror stories about dating apps. These media outlets are promoting love of self and perfection, whereas years ago life was about being yourself and enjoying the gifts God has given us. If we had a dollar for every "selfie" that was taken, we would all be rich. It is really affecting our children because they are trying to live up to expectations that are often impossible. King Solomon put it this way, "Vanity of vanities; all is vanity" (Ecclesiastes 1:2 KJV). Satan loves to see people strive for perfection because it is an unattainable goal. If he can get kids to take the bait, he can torment them for life.

Birds, on the other hand, are what they were created to be. When I first hung birdfeeders in my yard, I filled them with birdseed that many species of birds would like. I shortly realized that blackbirds are bully birds. They literally ate all the seed in a couple of days. Every day there were more blackbirds feasting in my yard. I spent time looking for different birdfeeders and researching seeds that they hated; once I found the right ones the blackbirds were history.

One day when I was reading my Bible, God showed me that how I feel about blackbirds, is the same way He feels about Satan. I was trying to feed the finches, chickadees, and cardinals, but the blackbirds would not allow them to eat. God tries to feed us wisdom about life; He wants us to know that He created us with gifts that nobody else has and we don't have to be like someone else. However, as soon as we get close to eating the words of truth that will nourish us, the devil appears and prevents us from digesting the words of encouragement. Satan immediately provides other feed for us that is full of low self-esteem and hopelessness. When we find ourselves in this situation, we need to seek daily God's natural nutritious meals and repel the synthetic diet that the enemy offers. As soon as Satan entices us with a taste of vanity or low self-esteem, we need to spit it out immediately and ask God to fill us with nuggets of encouragement.

BATTLE PLAN: Many of us have heard the saying, "The early bird catches the worm," meaning that if we rise early and work hard, we will be successful. Former president Franklin D. Roosevelt had a different perspective of this idiom; he said: "I think we consider too much the luck of the early bird and not enough of the bad luck of the early worm." You see, they both got up early; one was fed, and one was eaten. Everything in life is not clear cut. What works for some people does not work for other people. Yet, society is always promoting the *"one thing, or one method"* that will make us successful, happy, or popular. When we spend time with God by reading his word and praying, He will not only show us who we are, but He will give us a vision of who we can become. Don't let the enemy twist scripture to confuse you, which is one of his biggest weapons. He did this to Eve in the garden of Eden, so make sure you confirm scripture in the Bible if it is given to you by someone.

BATTLE SONG: "Simply Vanity" by Chris Howland

Sewing New Thoughts into Our Minds

"Do not conform to the pattern of this world, but be transformed by the renewing of your mind." —Romans 12:2 (NIV)

When God created nature, He also put in place the ability for natural regeneration to restore/replace damaged things. An example of this would be when a plant/tree dies in the forest, new seeds plant themselves and eventually replace the one that perished. Just like God perfectly orchestrated the timing of the moon or sun to rise, He put in place the amount of time it takes to regenerate nature.

Scientists and environmentalists have been assisting in the regeneration of nature, which isn't always a good thing because it can disrupt the ecosystem. Similarly, when God made human beings, He patterned their internal systems to work perfectly. Our brains have three main structures that work together to keep us alive. It also determines our personality, the way we think, and our emotions. While most doctors have humanity's best interest at heart, they often prescribe drugs that prohibit our brains from doing its job properly thus, altering our thoughts, dulling our emotions, and leaving us in an anesthetized state.

Working through the problems that cause depression can be difficult, especially if they were the result of a traumatic experience that we encountered. Before modern medicine was invented, people were forced to deal with the cruelties and devastation that life often brings. Perhaps this was easier because more people believed in God back then and put their trust in Him to help them overcome their dilemma. So, how do we get back to those days? The opening scripture states that we can get there by *"renewing our mind."*

BATTLE PLAN: Just like God's regeneration plan worked naturally for nature, His renewal plan for us should work the same, but it doesn't because we have an enemy snatching up the seeds of encouragement or regrowth that God is trying to sow in us. Evangelist Billy Sunday once said, "Temptation is the devil looking through the keyhole. Yielding is opening the door and inviting him in." Are we doing that? When scientists try to interfere with the regeneration of nature, they sometimes cause bigger problems. When we try to follow the patterns of the world instead of setting our "minds on things above, not on earthly things" (Colossians 3:2-3 NIV), we often do the same, which gives the devil access to our thoughts. The good thing is that even though we may give up on ourselves, God will never give up on us. He loves us and He is waiting for us to seek His words of life in the Bible, so He can encourage, strengthen, and renew our minds. So, let's make today the first day of the transformation process that will free us from the captivity of despair!

BATTLE SONG: "Made New" by Lincoln Brewster

BINDING FRIENDSHIPS

No matter how old we are, friends are an important part of our lives. There are people in my life who I have been friends with for decades. When I think of them, Proverbs 17:17 (NIV) comes to mind: "A friend loves at all times." This scripture doesn't mean that people don't argue, but rather that they lovingly work out their differences. These types of comfortable friendships are the ones that do hold us together when life is crazy and we are struggling, because we can totally be ourselves with them and not worry about being judged or betrayed.

King Solomon was known as the wisest man of his era. He said that "Two are better than one, because they have a good return for their labor: If either of them falls down, one can help the other up…though one may be overpowered, two can defend themselves. A cord of three strands is not quickly broken" (Ecclesiastes 4:9-10, 12 NIV). A friendship that has Jesus in the middle of it will last and be sturdy because the Lord is not going to let either one of the two in the friendship have peace if they are causing discord. The apostle Paul put it this way: "Carry each other's burdens, and in this way, you will fulfill the law of Christ" (Galatians 6:2 NIV). When we help others through difficulties, we are not only doing what Jesus commanded, but we are defeating Satan's plan to keep us in captivity. When Jesus was on the earth He said, "I no longer call you servants, because a servant does not know his master's business. Instead, I have called you friends, for everything that I learned from my Father I have made known to you" (John 15:15 NIV). When we find ourselves friendless during difficult times in our lives, Jesus knows how we feel because He was often alone in His suffering. He told His disciples, "Indeed the hour is coming, yes, has now come, that you will be scattered, each to his own, and will leave Me alone. And yet I am not alone because the Father is with Me" (John 16:32 NKJ). The Father is with us too; Jesus showed us His promises that are written in the Bible. It's up to us to search them out.

BATTLE PLAN: "Walk with the wise and become wise, for a companion of fools suffers harm" (Proverbs 13:20 NIV). If our "friends" scatter when we our going through difficulty, perhaps we have been hanging out with fools, or maybe our friends disappeared because we refuse to take their advice—even though they have conquered the enemy of despair. Satan loves when we refuse to help ourselves; he floods our minds with hopelessness and tries to separate us from the people trying to help us. This tear in the stitches holding our friendships together can begin to unravel; if not mended quickly, the stitches can become totally severed.

Some of Jesus' miraculous healings required that the person participate in their healing. One day Jesus and his disciples walked past a man who was blind. Jesus "spit on the ground, made some mud with the saliva, and put it on the man's eyes. 'Go, he told him, wash in the Pool of Siloam.' So, the man went and washed and came home seeing" (John 9:6-7). Jesus could have touched his eyes and healed them, but He made the blindman go to the pool and wash. The Bible does not state the reason why, but maybe Jesus wanted to see if he believed he could be healed. Our relationship with Jesus is a partnership; He wants to help us and sometimes our part in the healing is simply believing Him. "As iron sharpens iron, so one person sharpens another" (Proverbs 27:17 NIV). Sometimes God uses our friends to bring healing into our life, other times He want us to lay our burdens down.

BATTLE SONG: "Tim Tebow Song: Iron Sharpens Iron'" by Greg Davis

A TIME TO KEEP SILENT, AND A TIME TO SPEAK
—ECCLESTIASTES 3:7B

SILENCE IS GOLDEN

"We need to find God, and he cannot be found in noise and restlessness. God is the friend of silence. See how nature—trees, flowers, grass—grows in silence; see the stars, the moon and the sun, how they move in silence....We need silence to be able to touch souls." —Mother Teresa

In March of 2018, Southeastern Massachusetts was hit with three nor'easters in four weeks. The winds were extreme and there were trees down all over the place, which led to power outages. Months later, I was sitting on my patio enjoying the beautiful weather and I noticed a group of trees near the pool. The first three trees were all leaning on the last few trees, and the first tree was leaning the most. It had taken the brunt of the wind off the ocean during the winter storms. As the wind and snow pounded the first tree, it survived by leaning on the second tree; the second tree leaned on the third tree; and the third tree leaned on the fourth tree. If these trees were by themselves, they would have been uprooted by the powerful gales. However, because they were close together in a line, they all survived. The first few trees sheltered the last couple of trees from the wind. In doing so, they were now permanently bent over.

I thought about life and the damage we incur as we survive the storms that come our way. God showed me through these trees that it is okay to lean on others. Sometimes we feel like we must be strong and go it alone, but if these trees were by themselves, they would have perished. The trees in front would have been blown over, thus leaving the last few trees without protection, causing them to be uprooted as well. Luckily, trees do not have pride or the ability to reason like humans do. We tend to overthink things, and our society has taught us that we need to be self-sufficient—especially if you are a man. God warns us about this situation in His word: "Pride goes before destruction, and a haughty spirit before the fall" (Proverbs 16:18 NIV). Remember, the enemy of your soul will be cheering you on to go it alone because his goal is to totally destroy you. However, God wants us to live up to His standards and not the world's. Galatians 6:2 (NIV) says, "Carry each other's burdens, and in this way, you will fulfill the law of Christ." If we stay close to one another, like the trees, we have a better chance of surviving whatever comes our way, because the pressure is not on us alone.

BATTLE PLAN: We can learn so much from nature because God orchestrated everything to work perfectly. I am a visual learner, so seeing the trees was a huge awakening for me. Just as things in nature grow in silence, so do I. It is when I block out the noise around me that I can hear God's voice and see the lessons He wants to teach me through His beautiful creation. Where are you right now in the tempests of life? If you have been on the front lines for years taking the brunt of the wind and protecting others, perhaps it's time for you to lean on them. The trees lean naturally, and they flourish—I bet you will, too. If, however, you have been sheltered from the harsh realities of life, perhaps it is time for you to be an anchor for someone who has been injured in the storm. Whether you decide to lean on someone or be an anchor—seek God and He will give you the strength and guidance you need to do it!

BATTLE SONG: "Together" by For King and Country

THE SILENT & UNSEEN

"We do not look at the things which are seen, but at the things which are not seen."
—*2 Corinthians 4:18 (NKJ)*

There are so many things going on in the world that cause stress and fear; invasions, tornados, inflation are but a few to mention. Perhaps, we should be more concerned about the things we do not see, rather than the things we do see. Things hidden can be just as dangerous and maybe more severe because they take us by surprise. The ocean may be calm, and everything looks good; there are no enemy ships in sight and the sun is shining beautifully on the water while birds sit on top of it floating with the current. However, below the surface there is an enemy submarine that is hidden from radar and everyone and everything on it are totally silent, so they will not be discovered. When the order is given, missiles are fired strategically causing destruction and panic at the explosion site.

Things in the spiritual realm are very similar. In fact, Satan's biggest advantage is that some people do not even believe that he and his demons exist, and those who do might not realize how he uses people to accomplish his evil deeds. As with any enemy, there is an advantage in striking during the dead of night when people are alone and sleeping. The darkness intensifies the fear of the attack because we often can't tell where the weapons are coming from.

One of my brothers was crossing the street at night and was hit by a car. His injuries were extensive: a severed humerus bone, fractured ribs, collapsed lung, fractured pelvis, broken leg with all the ligaments torn and the other knee's ligaments were all torn, and a cracked xiphoid process. He was in the hospital and rehab for months and had several surgeries. When he was struck by the car, he landed on the hood of the car, hit the windshield, and landed twenty to thirty feet up the street. The amazing thing was that he did not have an injury to his head, not even a scratch. He never saw the car coming and the last thing he remembered was walking in the crosswalk.

My brother finally came home a couple of weeks after his last surgery and one of his neighbors described how they all heard my brother screaming in pain. One of the neighbors, who was a veteran,

ran outside into the street and held my brother's hand while they were waiting for the ambulance to show up. He was telling my brother to "stay with him" and my brother kept saying he couldn't. After my brother heard the story, he still could not remember the events because his brain was suppressing them. However, he began waking up in the middle of the night with fear. He didn't even know what he was afraid of—he was just afraid. He learned that reading a daily devotional or his Bible could help him handle the attacks. He also started taking a vitamin with ashwagandha in it. The attacks became less frequent, and finally disappeared totally. Fear can be conquered when we use the weaponry described in Ephesians 6 in the Bible. Believe God's promises and fight Satan with God's word to defeat him. I know that works because that is how Jesus fought against the devil in the desert (Matthew 4:1-11).

BATTLE STRATEGY: We must pray and ask God to help us fight the enemy. As Christians, we have the power of the risen Christ within us. 1 John 4:4 (KJV) says, "Greater is he that is in you, than he that is in the world." In the dead of the night when the enemy fills our mind with fear, we can command him to flee, in the name of Jesus. Putting Christian worship music on and praising God also helps us fight this spiritual battle; the enemy hates worship music, so he will flee.

BATTLE SONG: "Rescue" by Lauren Daigle

STOP COMPLAINING

"For Christ's love compels us, because we are convinced that one died for all, and therefore all died. And he died for all, that those who live should no longer live for themselves but for him who died for them and was raised again." —2 Corinthians 5:14-15 (NIV)

There are times in our lives when life is just too hard and we are beaten down. We finally think the storm is over and find the strength to get back up, only to be knocked back down by hurricane force winds. Sometimes the cycle continues, and we no longer have the desire to go on. I was in a season of my life that I was tired of the fight. After complaining about my situation to God, I read my Bible and some devotionals. Instead of God disciplining me for whining, He led me somewhere in His word that encouraged me and reminded me that He was beside me in the battle. This compelled me to persevere. In hindsight, I saw that God always had a purpose for the storms in my life, and He worked them together for my good and the good of others.

It was during the times when the waves were overpowering me that God was using me as a vessel to bring somebody to Him. Some people watched as I kept afloat through the stormy seas of cancer, others saw forgiveness when the ominous winds of abuse hit me, while some observed the unstable clouds of my finances and the blessings that followed. Witnessing God's faithfulness to not only get me through, but to also bring all kinds of healing was the catalyst for people to accept Jesus as their savior. They finally realized that I was telling the truth when I said that I was not a strong person, but that "I can do everything through Christ, who gives me strength" (Philippians 4:13 NLT). I never would have survived the storms without the Lord!

Jesus said, "Come to Me, all you who are weary and burdened, and I will give you rest. Take my Yoke upon you and learn from me, for I am gentle and humble in heart, and you will find rest for your souls. For my yoke is easy and my burden is light" (Matthew 11:28-30 NIV). According to Dictionary.com, a yoke is "a device for joining together a pair of draft animals, especially oxen, usually consisting of a crosspiece with two bow-shaped pieces, each enclosing the head of an animal." As such, one animal is not carrying the heavy burden by itself. It is important to notice why Jesus used this example: He was telling us that we *will* have burdens, we *will* grow weary, but *His* yoke lightens those burdens. Some people believe that when they become a Christian all their problems will disappear. On the contrary, our trials usually intensify because we are now a threat to the devil's kingdom, so his attacks increase. This shouldn't be hard to understand; someone in the military is under attack more than a civilian. however, they are also trained to fight and are prepared for the battle. Are you armed and ready to fight?

BATTLE PLAN: The deeper we grow in our walk with God, the more we become aware of the battle of good and evil around us. Now more than ever we can see the evidence of darkness in the world. Not thinking about life after death does not change the fact that we will all spend eternity somewhere. However, when we no longer live for ourselves and live for God's kingdom, our burdens on Earth will be lighter because we will be yoked together with Jesus. It will be His strength that carries and guides us. When our life is over, we will spend eternity in heaven, where there are no more tears or sorrow. Until then, if we keep our focus on God and not our problems, He can use us to advance His kingdom and encourage others.

BATTLE SONG: "It's Not Over Yet" by For King & Country

THE COURAGE TO SPEAK

"What counts is not necessarily the size of the dog in the fight—it's the size of the fight in the dog."— *President Dwight D. Eisenhower*

Part of growing up in an Italian family is learning how to voice your opinion. Some of us never learned the "inside voice" concept. My mom was Lithuanian, and her parents never raised their voices. In fact, when my parents got married, they moved in with my dad's mom. One of my uncles and his family lived there as well. Every night at the dinner table there was an argument, and my mom broke out in hives because she got so nervous however, she eventually got used to it. The funny thing is that family members could be arguing and yelling to make their point and when they were each done, one would say something like, *hey pass the salt* and everyone would laugh. One would think that these skills were not useful, but they helped me accomplish a task when I was in Uganda with Carrie and Edith.

A school for the deaf that we visited needed renovations for the children's dorms. That was not part of our agenda, but we contacted people in the US to raise donations for the supplies needed to do the dorms over. We raised enough money to buy paint, beds, mattresses, sheets, blankets, Bibles, and mosquito nets. One day our driver, Adolph, drove Carrie and me to Kampala to purchase the beds. We had already purchased the mattresses, which were on a truck that was following us. God faithfully provided a parking spot right in front of the store and the beds were outside on the grass. We found the beds we wanted, but some of them lacked paint in areas. I told the man helping us that the spots needed to be painted before I paid for the beds. As we waited, the man driving the truck with the mattresses went to park somewhere and Adolf walked up the street to get lunch. Carrie and I were in the car and the owner of the store started knocking on the window telling me to move the car because he needed the parking spot. I cracked the window and told him that I couldn't move the car and he started yelling; people in the street stopped and were looking at us. I got out of the car and told Carrie to lock the door. I told the man that I didn't have a license to drive in Uganda, but he didn't care and kept insisting I move the car. My Italian descent kicked in, and I told him that he could yell all he wanted to, but I was NOT moving the car because I was still a customer waiting for the beds. I got in the car and locked the door; he eventually walked away and so did the spectators. We got the beds when they were ready, and we went on our way. God used my Italian boldness, to accomplish my mission that day. When God sends us somewhere, He makes sure that we are equipped for the mission, just like any commander would. In life, we have a choice to fight for something or give in. The choice we makes determines the outcome of our situation. God want us to have abundant life, but we have to want it as well. When we choose to fight against whatever is oppressing us, God can help us.

BATTTLE PLAN: Animals and most people will come out fighting when they are backed into a corner Someone who is trying to help them is often mistaken for an enemy; examples of this are a dog catcher or someone trying to help a person drowning. Sometimes the rescuer must stay a safe distance away until the fight in the animal or person is gone. Sometimes God takes a step back when we need help because we are fighting Him instead of accepting His help. Anxiety and depression can be so overwhelming, and it is a hard battle to fight on our own. Remember God is not the enemy, Satan is. We must stop fighting our rescuer and let Him help us to victory!

BATTLE SONG: "Fear is a Liar" by Zach Williams

WHEN GOD SPEAKS TO OUR HEART

"God speaks in the silence of the heart." —*Mother Teresa*

Have you ever been lost and had no idea which way to go, but your intuition was telling you to drive or walk in a certain direction and it turns out to be the right way? That is God speaking to your spirit and showing you the way in which you should walk (Isaiah 30:21). Have you ever been betrayed by someone you love, and you were devasted? As you cry, the thought comes to your mind that you're better off without this person? Perhaps God is guiding you to see the truth (John 16:13). Maybe you have drifted away from God and out of nowhere you begin wondering how you got so far away from Him; this is God speaking to your heart telling you to come back to Him (John 14:26).

Has there ever been a time in your life that you felt like you couldn't go on anymore and suddenly your mood changes and you decide to fight whatever is holding you captive? This is God giving you the desire to persevere. King Solomon said, "The King's heart is in the hand of the LORD, like the rivers of water, He turns it wherever He wishes" (Proverb 21:1 NKJ). God speaks through actions as well. Have you ever been so sick that all you can do is lie in bed and cry; suddenly, you fall asleep and sleep for hours (Isaiah 29:10)? This is God carrying you through your suffering. Has God been speaking to your heart lately? If so, are your listening and following His guidance?

BATTLE PLAN: C. S. Lewis once said, "Once people stop believing in God, the problem is not that they believe in nothing; rather, the problem is that they will believe anything." We must be careful of the voices speaking to our hearts and minds because the devil can also send thoughts and desires our way. Therefore, it is important for us to make sure that it is actually God who is speaking to us through His Holy Spirit. We can do this by making sure that our thoughts, impulses, or actions line up with God's word in the Bible. The apostle John wrote: "Dear friends, do not believe every spirit, but test the spirits to see whether they are from God; because many false prophets have gone out into the world" (1 John 4:1 NIV). God will never tell us to do something that contradicts His words in the Bible. Sometimes our desires line up with His word, but we still aren't sure if it is the Lord's will for us. Asking God to fill us with His peace to confirm that He wants us to proceed in a certain direction is also helpful. If we still are not sure what God is telling us to do, we should pray and wait for His confirmation.

BATTLE SONG: "I Will Follow" by Chris Tomlin

FRAGRANT WORDS

"Now thanks be to God who always leads us in triumph in Christ, and through us diffuses the fragrance of His knowledge in every place. For we are to God the fragrance of Christ among those who are being saved and among those who are perishing." —2 Corinthians 2:14-15 (NKJV)

Fragrant flowers, plants, and herbs have been around since the beginning of time. They are used to make incense, anointing oil, medicine, creams, shampoos, deodorizers, perfume, and many other things. The Bible tells us that we should "walk in love" like Jesus did and be a "fragrant aroma" as a sacrifice to God, and to be used for His purpose. (Ephesians 5:1-2). As much as we try to be a sweet-smelling aroma for the Lord, we often fail. We must remember that all God's children sin and fall short of His glory, yet God still forgives us. He wants us to forgive ourselves, so that we can move on to a new season of our lives.

Our sense of smell connects to nerves in our brain that triggers emotions. A pleasant scent can bring positive feelings, while a rotten odor can trigger negative vibes. Therefore, it is so important for Christians to exhibit the true essence of Christ's love—one that will attract people to Him because it sprouts blossoms of truth, hope, and encouragement. Sometimes God's children water down the fragrance of His words, or release an overpowering aroma of scripture, which causes people to flee. The next time they encounter the scent, it triggers memories of what that smell represents, and they do not want to be near it. If you have been a victim of that, please do not associate people's actions with who Jesus is—He is the best friend you will ever have, and his fragrance of love, compassion, and healing are like none other.

Perfume can be extremely expensive and often used by the purchaser sparingly on special occasions. Many people purchase knockoff brands of their favorite fragrance that they use daily because it is cheaper. However, people who have smelled the "real" perfume can recognize the imitation. Our witness of God's love works in a similar manner. If our words do not line up with our actions, people usually assume that we are a "knockoff" Christian, one that preaches,

241

but does not live out the sermon. Jesus said, "The very works that I do—bear witness of Me, that the Father has sent Me" (John 5:36b). We need to ask ourselves, what fragrance are we diffusing to a world full of lost and hurting people?

BATTLE PLAN: Since God tells us in His word. "There is no one righteous, not even one" (Romans 3:10 NIV), we are going to have times of weakness when we fall short of the mark. Depression is one of those enemies that attacks and sucks the life out of us. We often stop engaging with people and sometimes we don't even want to take a shower. During these times we need to take hold of *"the fragrance of His knowledge."* Christ can lead us to victory because He experienced what we are going through, but we need to seek His wisdom and implement it. Once we are healed Jesus can diffuse His scent of love, peace, and joy through us. The enemy is sly and will always be on the prowl trying to get us off track. Therefore, we need to always evaluate ourselves. When we are near people, do they smell God's aroma, or is the scent weakened with elements of compromise that we outwardly exhibit? Are we talking to others about the joy of the Lord, but our scents of bitterness and unforgiveness rather than love and mercy are exhibited? If so, it is time to start wearing the authentic fragrance of Christ, or no fragrance at all. Charles Spurgeon once said, "The bible contains Jesus Christ's letters to us, perfumed by His love." If we are called to be" Christ's ambassadors" (2 Corinthians 5:20), then our fragrance must be like His—it's never too late to throw out the watered-down fragrance and wear the real thing!

BATTLE SONG: "So Long Self" by Mercy Me

GOD SPEAKS IN MANY WAYS

"I love to think of nature as an unlimited broadcasting station through which God speaks to us every hour, if we will only tune in."— *George Washington Carver*

Many people over the years have asked me how I know that God is telling me to do something or not to do something. My first response is to say that the Bible is the written word of God, and He speaks to me through His word, which He does. However, God also communicates with me through nature

The book of Genesis 1 states that God "spoke" the heavens and the earth into existence, so why wouldn't He use creation to open our eyes and ears to hear what He wants to say to us? If we look at what is going on in nature, we will see God's hand in everything. Animals gathering food before an approaching storm tells us that if God put that instinct in them, He will warn us as well of an upcoming tempest. A spring flower blooming in the snow is a symbol of perseverance, and if we are diligent and don't give up, we can rise above adversity, too. The amazing beauty of the daily sunrise and sunset is a reminder that tomorrow will be a new day with a fresh start and yesterday is in the past. Sometimes God speaks to our souls through his still small voice. Yet, other times, God speaks to us through a friend or even a stranger. Has that ever happened to you? I think we can agree that God is everywhere trying to catch our attention and talk to us. It is when we open our eyes and ears to see and hear Him that our lives will be blessed with His encouragement, peace, and love!

BATTLE PLAN: The Bible tells us that "God saw all that he had made and it was very good" (Genesis 1:31 NIV). He made people in His image and blessed them (Genesis 1:28) because He loves us. Why would He go through all that effort just to abandon us and not help us? He wouldn't, actually we are the ones who walk away from Him. When we find it hard to believe that God loves us, we need to take a walk outside and *"tune in"* to our surroundings. When we do, we will hear and see all the beauty and good things He has provided for us. If we ask Him to speak to us through His creation, He will!

243

BATTLE SONG: "Everything" by TobyMac

A TIME TO BE SILENT

"Go out and stand on the mountain before the LORD. And behold, the LORD passed by, and a great and strong wind tore into the mountains and broke the rocks in pieces before the LORD, but the LORD was not in the wind; and after the wind an earthquake, but the LORD was not in the earthquake; and after the earthquake a fire, but the LORD was not in the fire; and after the fire a still small voice." —1 Kings 19:11-12 (NKJ)

Some people believe that God is always angry and that He speaks to us in claps of thunder and bolts of lightning. When I was a child, I was afraid of thunder and lightning; my mom told me that thunder was the noise that God made when He was bowling in Heaven. Every time there was an extremely loud crack of thunder it meant that God got a strike and the rumbles after were the pins falling down. This comforted me in many ways, because it not only gave me a reason for the loud noises, but it made me smile to think that God was having fun bowling. I liked to bowl, so I felt that we had something in common. Life seemed simpler back then; on Sunday, the stores were closed and most people did not work, they rested. Even God rested on the seventh day after creating the heavens and the earth. Scripture doesn't say that He had to rest, but that He did rest. Nowadays, people are so busy with all the latest technology they are constantly listening to some type of noise. How can they possibly hear God's still small voice like the prophet Elijah did in the opening scripture? What if God is trying to warn us about something?

Elijah was by himself in a quiet cave when he was instructed to go to the mountain. The instructions he received on the mountain were very important and he never would have heard them if he was constantly in a noisy environment. It is so important for us to get away from the noise and busyness of life, so that we can hear God speak to us.

BATTLE PLAN: Psalm 46:10 (NLT) says, "Be *still*, and know that I am God!" However, when the world around us appears to be falling apart, we often feel like we need to do something to fix it. We watch the news, ask people for advice, research things, and when we are out

245

of options, we then turn to God in silent prayer and ask for wisdom. Maybe if we had sought God first, He would have prepared us for what was coming, and we could have avoided the anxiety we felt. This doesn't mean that God is always going to tell us what will happen in the future, but that He will reminds us that He is in control of everything and there is nothing to fear, because He is not only with us—He loves us!

BATTLE SONG: "Word of God Speak" by MercyMe

SPEAKING BOLDLY TO THE GIANTS BEFORE US

"My soul silently waits for God alone, for my expectation is from Him. He only is my rock and my salvation; He is my defense. I shall not be moved." —Psalm 62:5-6 (NKJ)

In the opening scripture. David is escaping from those who were out to get him. He puts his trust in God as he waits for Him to deal with his enemies. If you didn't know David's history, you may think that he is hiding because he is a coward who is fearful, but that is not the case.

David was anointed king when he was just a shepherd boy, but it was not God's time for him to take the throne. This is the same David who took out the mighty giant Goliath, with a sling shot. This is the description of Goliath as stated in 1 Samuel 17:4-7 (NLT): "He was over nine feet tall! He wore a bronze helmet, and his bronze coat of mail weighed 125 pounds. He also wore bronze leg armor, and he carried a bronze javelin oh his shoulder. The shaft of the spear was as heavy and thick as a weaver's beam, tipped with an iron spearhead that weighed 15 pounds." Saul's soldiers couldn't defeat Goliath because they were terrified of him, and it was a boy with a stone and a sling shot that took him down.

God had been preparing David for that day for years. As a shepherd, he became proficient with a sling shot while he was protecting his sheep in the field from lions and bears. However, there is also another reason for the shepherd boy's victory that day. When Goliath told David that he was going to feed his flesh to the birds, David's response was: "You come to me with a sword, spear and a javelin, but I come to you in the name of the LORD of Heaven's Armies—the God of the armies of Israel, whom you have defiled. Today the LORD will conquer you and I will kill you...this is the LORD'S battle" (1 Samuel 17:45-47 NLT). David's skill with his sling shot and his faith in God's promise to be with him, gave him the courage to be a warrior. What giants are you facing today? Are you putting your faith and trust in God to deliver you?

BATTLE PLAN: Throughout our lives we will face giants, some of them may be physical and others may be the ones in our mind: fear, depression, or hopelessness. The important thing to take away from David's story is that David was just doing his job as a shepherd, he had no idea that God was training him to be a warrior and the king of Israel. As a shepherd, David counted on God to help him kill the lions and bears that were attacking his flock, so he believed that God would give him the victory against Goliath. However, it was His verbal proclamation to Goliath, that also secured the victory. It showed God that David truly believed His promises and when God came through for David, all the soldiers of the Israeli army witnessed God's faithfulness as well. If we reflect on our life, perhaps we can see that the enemies we fought in the past prepared us for the giants we are facing today. Just like David used the sling shot, we must use weapons that we fought with in the past to defeat the giants we are facing today. The force behind all the giants is Satan, he just wears different uniforms to disguise himself. Remember that God is much more powerful than the devil, so we must boldly proclaim to the giant we are facing that we *come in the name of the Lord and the battle is His. Today He will deliver you into my hand!*

BATTLE SONG: "Confidence" by Sanctus Real

248

A TIME TO LOVE, AND A TIME TO HATE—ECCLESIASTES 3:8A

God's Unconditional Love

"He returned home to his father. And while he was still a long way off, his father saw him coming. Filled with love and compassion, he ran to his son, embraced him, and kissed him." —Luke 15:20 (NLT)

When Jesus wanted the people to know how deep His Father's love was for them, He told them a story about "The Lost Son" (Luke 15:11-32). The father in the story had two sons. His youngest son asked for and was given his inheritance, even though his dad was still alive. Once he received his share of the estate, he traveled to other countries and eventually spent all the money. He found himself hungry with no means to buy food. It was in this place of despair that he remembered how well his father's servants were fed, so he decided that he would go home and ask his dad for forgiveness and a job.

The son never expected his father to greet him so lavishly and celebrate his return with music and a feast! The boy said to his dad, "Father, I have sinned against both heaven and you, and I am no longer worthy of being called your son" (Luke 15:21 NLT). The father told his servants, "Quick! Bring the finest robe in the house and put it on him. Get a ring for his finger and sandals for his feet. And kill the calf we have been fattening. We must celebrate with a feast for this son of mine was dead and has now returned to life. He was lost, but now he is found" (Luke 15:22-24 NLT). This story is an example of what grace is: getting what you don't deserve.

This is how God feels when one of His children returns to Him saying, *"I am sorry I have sinned against you, please forgive me."* I can just imagine the celebration in heaven when one of God's children repents of their sins and comes back to Him. Just like the dad in the story didn't rehash what transpired and how it hurt him, but instead celebrated his return, God will do the same when one of his children repents. Our heavenly Father never gives up hope that one of His prodigals will return. Perhaps we know what this feels like because one of our children has left home and we don't know where they are. The best thing we can do is pray and never give up hope.

God wants your child to return home, too! If you are the prodigal one, don't let pride or shame keep you from coming home and claiming your inheritance! If you are the angry sibling, rejoice and be glad for the return of your brother/sister's return. Remember, God has enough love and blessings for all His children.

BATTLE STRATEGY: There is some truth to the old adage the grass is always greener on the other side of the fence. If someone just saw the beginning of the prodigal son's venture away from his father and witnessed the child having fun and traveling the world, they would think the grass was truly greener on the other side. However, if they saw the whole story played out and the part where the prodigal son was in the field feeding the pigs and he was contemplating eating the pig's pods because he was so hungry, they would realize that there is no truth to the saying. Satan's goal is to entice you away with half-truths. He will make sure that your preview of "happiness" is everything you are looking for. However, the truth is that things are not always what they appear to be. Don't fall for the lies of the enemy. If you have already ventured out, run back home to your Father in heaven who is waiting to celebrate your return!!

BATTLE SONG: "Prodigal" by Casting Crowns

THE LION & THE LAMB

In the 1950's Author C. S. Lewis wrote a book series called *The Chronicles of Narnia*, which was made into a film series in 2005. In both, Aslan the lion was the real king of Narnia and a symbol for Jesus Christ. In the first film, Aslan dies sacrificially, but then resurrects. He comes back to life and saves his people. Real lions, however, only take care of those in their pride (a group of lions like a pack) and once the male cubs turn two years old, they are forced to leave the pride. These cubs roam by themselves looking for a pride to join. When they find one, they fight the male lion in it until one of them dies. If the leader of the pride dies, the victorious lion will kill all the male cubs in the pride.

The animal kingdom is very different from God's kingdom. The name alone for a group of lions, "pride," illustrates this. If you were to google synonyms for the word pride you would find words like self-importance, dignity, arrogance etc. These words describe the male lions perfectly—they want to be "king of the jungle." Jesus is the total opposite: humble, meek, and of no reputation. He came as a sacrificial lamb to suffer and die for our sins because He loves us.

Jesus is currently seated at the right hand of the Father in heaven and intercedes for us (Romans 8:34). Psalm 34:10 (NIV) says, "The young lions may grow weak and hungry, but those who seek the LORD lack no good thing." Therefore, if we pray and we do not receive what we want, there is a chance that what we think is good for us really isn't, or maybe it is but the timing is wrong. Perhaps our prayers are being ignored because what we want may turn us into prideful lions or cause us to be thrown out of the pack because of our pride. We may never know the answers to our questions until we die, or until Jesus comes back to get us.

Jesus came to the earth the first time as a lamb but will come the second time as a lion/warrior (Revelation 5:5, 19:11-16). He said before he left Earth, "Let not your heart be troubled; you believe in God, believe also in Me. In My Father's house are many mansions; if it were not so, I would have told you. I go to prepare a place for you. And if I go and prepare a place for you, I will come again and receive you to Myself; that where I am, there you may be also. And where I go you know, and the way you know (John 14:1-4 NKJ). This should give us all some peace and comfort when the world and those in it are causing us pain

BATTLE PLAN: The Bible states that nobody knows the day or hour of Jesus' return (Matthew 24). However, when the Lord was on Earth, He talked to the people in parables (stories) giving examples of how we need to be prepared for His return. The birth pains of the signs that the time is near are currently evident for all to see (Matthew 24:39-39 and 1Thessalonians 4:13-5:3). The question all of us need to ask ourselves is, "Are we ready?" If not, it should be our top priority.

BATTLE SONGS: "I Will Rise" by Chris Tomlin & "Lion" by Elevation Worship

WHAT OR WHO COMPELS US

"For Christ's love compels us." — *2 Corinthians 5:14 (NIV)*

The apostle Paul wrote the opening scripture, which was in a letter sent to the church of Corinth. He heard rumors that sin was infiltrating the church and he was concerned. Paul totally understood the concept of grace, as well as how to turn from your sinful ways. His life changing "road to Damascus" experience turned his life completely around. It was Christ's love and forgiveness that compelled the murderous Pharisee to become one of Jesus's most dedicated advocates, and he advanced the gospel mightily. Although that was thousands of years ago, Christians all over the world gain wisdom and encouragement from Paul's words today.

The spiritual battle between good and evil will continue until the end of time. New fads, technology, and science can be great things, but they can also pull us away from the Lord—it is a slow fad that disguises itself as wisdom. Don't get me wrong there are so many technical and scientific discoveries that are good for us, and we need to thank God for them. The ones that deal with a person's thoughts and heart, however, should be embraced very cautiously.

Over the past decade, the younger generation is relying more and more on technology to take care of their day-to-day responsibilities. Psychological tests have been developed to help people understand themselves and others better. People can learn what motivates them and why they behave a certain way. This allows each person in the relationship to not only consider the other person's feelings, but to know exactly what encourages themselves or makes them feel loved. Many years ago, a book called the *5 Love Languages* was published that illustrated a similar concept. It had some great ideas, but made people want to be understood even more.

Jesus was totally misunderstood by people. He came to be a sacrificial lamb, not a king. He washed the disciple's feet the night before He was crucified as an example of how we should act. God loves us and has blessed everyone with their own unique gifts to make a difference in His kingdom. There are going to be times when He compels us to do something by squeezing and pressuring us. When we try to prevent or fix that from happening to someone else because we understand what makes them happy, we can be interfering with God's plans. The person feeling the pressure can feel hurt, offended, or angry when we don't try to make things better (even if they are wrong). They may list off attributes of their personality type and use that as an excuse for their bitterness or rudeness. Jesus never focused on who He was or what His needs were—He focused on us!! So, let's use the gift of technology and psychology to help us understand and serve others better and not ourselves.

BATTLE PLAN: Satan loves it when human's get offended, depressed, or angry. When we are in this state of self-absorption, we don't even notice the needs of people arounds us—who might be much worse off than us. Ironically, when our mind is on others and not ourselves, we tend to forget about our own problems. We all have something to offer others; if we cannot physically help them, we can still pray and encourage them. Imagine if *everyone* served others, the personality/love language concept would happen automatically because it would be Christ compelling us, not human wisdom!

BATTLE SONG: "Lifesong" by Casting Crowns

SACRIFICE & HONOR

"If a commission by an earthly king is considered an honor, how can a commission by a Heavenly King be considered a sacrifice?" —David Livingstone

Most of us view sacrifice as an obligation or something we do for our family, friends, or boss. Sometimes we don't mind giving up our time or money because we love the person asking. We may serve at church or in our community because it's the "right" thing to do. Sometimes if someone with status in these places asks us to take on a project that will require our constant attention and a lot of our time, we feel honored that we are chosen to carry out their vision and work with/for someone in a high position. Once we start the project, the time spent, the stress, and the heavy workload doesn't feel like a burden. We are often excited to get to know some "famous" people on a more personal level or perhaps elevate our worldly status, so that we can put a great achievement on our resume. If we could only have this attitude when it comes to serving the King of Kings and the Lord of Lords, Jesus! Fulfilling God's commission should not be accomplished with the attitude: "oh well, someone has to do it!" Each act of service should be viewed as an opportunity to get to know the Lord better and advance His agenda, not ours.

When we find ourselves apathetic towards God's calling, it could be because God is not asking us to perform that task, or it might be because we don't enjoy doing that type of work. The closer our relationship is with our heavenly King the more in tune we are with *our* purpose in *His* plan. When we accept a mission from Him, we will be excited to see how He will use us and hopefully we will be honored to be given the opportunity to be part of His team. Asking God to align our desires with His and opening and shutting the door to His will is giving our heavenly King permission to use us whenever He wants to. It also takes the guess work out of what His will is. God will equip us with all we need to accomplish the mission, which in turn, will build our faith and trust in Him. Since our desires are aligned with God's, our commission will not be sacrificial, but rather an honor. In addition, we will gain treasures in heaven.

BATTLE PLAN: Parents often assign chores and ask their children to do things that they do not like to do. This teaches their kids that life is not all about their happiness and that it involves hard work, commitment, and sacrifice. Children that are taught this at a young age are prepared for adulthood and responsibility. King Solomon once said, "I have seen the burden God has placed on us all. Yet God has made everything beautiful for its own time. He has planted eternity in the human heart, but even so, people cannot see the whole scope of God's working from beginning to end" (Ecclesiastes 3:10-11 NLT). Just like children cannot understand why parents make them work hard, we do not understand God's purpose for doing things. One thing that we do know is that He loves us, and He wants us to gain entrance into heaven when we die. Therefore, let's honor God with our service because He is using it to prepare us for eternity!

BATTLE SONG: "Best of Me" by Jordan Feliz

LOVE NEVER FAILS

"Do you see this woman? I came into your house; you did not give me any water for My feet, but she wet my feet with her tears and wiped them with her hair. You did not give me a kiss, but this woman has not stopped kissing my feet. You did not put oil on my head, but she has poured perfume on my feet. Therefore, I tell you, her many sins have been forgiven—as her great love has shown. But whoever has been forgiven little loves little." —Luke 7:44-47 (NIV)

When I met my first husband, I was twenty years old and worked at his father's restaurant. He was married and I was engaged. I loved God, prayed, and believed that Jesus died for my sins; however, I only went to church on Christmas and Easter. I had never read the Bible or even realized that I was saved by grace (Jesus' death on the cross). It was all about being a "good person," but what was considered good? When you are raised in that kind of environment you tend to compare yourself to other people to judge *your goodness.* I knew that committing adultery was a sin, but I thought if the person was separated from their spouse, they weren't really married. Through a series of events, I discovered that my fiancé was living another life that I knew nothing about and called off my wedding, and my first husband left his wife. At that time, we just occasionally talked at work. However, we began to talk more and more, which led to us dating. They eventually got divorced and we got married when I was twenty-three years old.

My husband and his ex-wife had a beautiful daughter together, so I would see her at family parties; one of those parties was our nephew's wedding. I noticed his ex-wife sitting by herself, so I invited her to come over and sit with us and she did. After that, I started inviting her to my house for some family gatherings and we became friends. We even played golf together and sometimes she would have dinner at my house. At the age forty-eight, she died of breast cancer and I was so upset. She was an amazing woman! God used her in my life to show me what grace really was, forgiveness when you don't deserve it. Since I totally understood the concept of grace and forgiveness, I was able to extend grace and forgive many people that hurt me throughout my life.

BATTLE PLAN: The difference between the woman with the fragrant oil and the Pharisee, Simon, in the opening scripture was that she knew she was a sinner and needed forgiveness. The Pharisee on the other hand, thought he was so righteous, and he *was*—on the outside. His heart on the inside was not pure, so Jesus pointed that out, whereas the woman's love for Christ covered a multitude of sins (1 Peter 4:8). She took her greatest treasure, the expensive oil, and anointed His feet with it. The Lord's Prayer says, "And forgive us our debts, as we also have forgiven our debtors (Matthew 6:12 NIV). That means that God is going to forgive us according to how we forgive others. I want God's forgiveness, do you? If you feel that you have done things that God could never forgive you for, you are wrong. In God's eyes sin, is sin; one sin isn't worse than another. Because of Jesus' love and sacrifice, our sins are forgiven when we repent. Therefore, when we need forgiveness, we just need to ask God for it and repent. We also must forgive others when they sin against us; remembering Luke 7 and Matthew 6, will encourage us to do the right thing. God wants to forgive us, and He is waiting for us to come to His throne of grace!

BATTLE SONG: "O Come to the Altar" by Elevation Worship

LOVING YOUR ENEMIES

"Love your enemies, do good to those who hate you." —Luke 6:27 (NIV)

I once read a story about a Christian who was living in a communist country and sent to prison for sharing the gospel. He was beaten repeatedly, only to have brief times in between beatings to heal a little before the next abuse began. The guard did not want to kill him but wanted him to live and suffer. Most of us would probably be asking God why He was allowing this torture rather than rewarding us for preaching the Gospel. However, this pastor knew the truth of Jesus' words and the effectiveness of them.

One day, the guard was beating the pastor and threatening to kill him. The preacher's response amazed me! He told his persecutor that God created him to do better things than inflict pain. Those words haunted the guard and he eventually accepted Jesus as his savior.

The Old Testament of the Bible taught that you should give "life for life, an eye for an eye and a tooth for a tooth" (Exodus 21:23). Basically, the sentence for those committing the crime was having the same affliction done to them. This sounds reasonable and was probably pretty effective in keeping the crime rate low. However, when Jesus came to Earth to die for our sins, His gift of salvation was offered to everyone. Normally, it is hard to be abusive to those who continually bless us. That doesn't mean it doesn't happen because it does; some people are just pure evil. There are those, however, that realize their actions are wrong and they don't want to be the person that they have become, like the guard in the story. When we bless those who curse us it gives God the opportunity to work in the persecutors heart, making it difficult for them to justify their actions. When the evil within us is revealed, it can be shocking to us.

I was physically abused by someone I trusted and loved. When I sought God for answers and guidance, all I got was "love your enemies." I asked God to love this person through me because I was filled with fear, bitterness, and resentment—God did exactly that; I was able to take care of this person when he was diagnosed with terminal cancer. Like the guard, he ended up surrendering his life to the Lord before he died. We were both set free. It was by letting God's love flow through me that I was healed; I was set free from the pain and bitterness that was hardening my heart. God's ways are not our ways—but they are the best ways! Do you need to let go of an injustice from the past? If so, ask God for guidance and wisdom.

BATTLE PLAN: The spirit of rage is straight from the pit of hell; when it attaches itself to a human, it takes control of their actions. Sometimes the person housing the rage feels awful and has remorse for their actions, but many times the person who inflicts the pain turns around and says that the person they attacked did something that caused their behavior. When this happens, Satan gets a two for one deal: the attacker stays as an abuser and the victim is filled with pain, fear, and bitterness. Jesus knew this would be the outcome and that is why He calls us to love our enemies, because "love covers over a multitude of sins" (1 Peter 4:8 NIV). Only God can work in someone's heart and reveal to them the evil that is in it. Therefore, we must turn to Him and pray for guidance regarding our situation and obey what He tells us to do. He may give different advice to someone in the same situation and tell them to forgive but leave the person. We also need to watch out for the attacks from the devil; he will do everything he can to make sure the relationship stays very volatile. Only God can bring healing to both people involved.

BATTLE SONG: "Ceasefire" by For King & Country

HATE WHAT IS EVIL

"The world is a dangerous place, not because of those who do evil, but because of those who look on and do nothing." —*Albert Einstein*

War is terrible, but sometimes a necessary thing. Since there is and will be evil in the world until the end of time, there will always be a battle going on against good and evil. The choice to go to war is always a hard decision. As such, many countries didn't get involved when Hitler started his conquest until it was evident that he might take control of the world. In fact, America didn't even know that they were at war with Japan until the Japanese attacked Pearl Harbor and killed thousands of sailors. As people saw the planes approaching the Hawaiian Islands, they had no idea what was going on. The same thing often happens in spiritual warfare. We have jets of hopelessness and fear entering our mind and we have no idea where they are coming from and why they are there. Just like American's didn't know that the Japanese planes were going to release bombs and cause catastrophes, people don't know that spiritual warfare is real and that Satan is out to destroy them.

The enemy of our soul likes to fly under the radar, like Japan did, and catch us off guard when we least expect it. Although Satan is the catalyst that starts physical wars, he does most of his damage waging war in the minds of people. If he can get us to believe his lies, he can easily overpower us. In hindsight, we wonder how Hitler fooled so many people. It was because he got them to believe his lies; he appeared to be doing what was best for the people, but he was evil. "Satan disguises himself as an angel of light" (2 Corinthians 2:14 NLT), which means that sometimes he acts like he is promoting good when actually, he is causing division in families, friends, and nations—just look at the divide in America today. The Bible calls us to "hate evil" (Psalm 97:10 NLT). Therefore, we need to seek out the truth because things are not always what they appear to be. United States Army officer Frederik W. Robert said, "I will tell you what to hate. Hate Hypocrisy; hate can't, hate intolerance; oppression, injustice, Pharisaism, hate them as Christ hated them—with a deep, abiding, God-like hatred." When we use this list as a guide, we are able to determine when the underlying force behind actions is Satan. People often choose to ignore the injustices and evil they see, which Einstein says is the reason we have a dangerous world. It was because people looked on and did nothing that Hitler was able to get away with his horrific deeds. Similarly, when we choose not to believe that there is a spiritual war going on, we allow the devil to get away with torturing our minds. Jesus conquered the same demons that taunt our thoughts and emotions. Therefore, when we follow His battle strategies, we will look at our problems and suffering from a different perspective and rise above our circumstances.

BATTLE PLAN: Dwight D. Eisenhower once said, "Neither a wise nor a brave man lies down on the tracks of history to wait for the train of the future to run over him." The enemy of our soul wants to keep us in the bondage of our past, so that we will have *no* future. If we wouldn't physically lie down on train tracks waiting for a train to kill us, why do we so willingly lie down on the emotional tracks that can mentally kill us? We must learn the enemies' tactics, so we are able to construct a battle plan to defeat him. We must never underestimate the enemy. Satan is powerful, but God is more powerful, and He will help us win the battle if we ask Him to.

BATTLE SONG: "New Day" by Danny Gokey

COMMITMENT & LOYALTY

"The true soldier fights not because he hates what is in front of him, but because he loves what is behind him." —G.K. Chesterton

What is love? Many describe it as a feeling, while others describe it as a sacrifice. The level of love we have for people can be different; our love for our spouse is different than our love for our children or our parents. We can also love our friends, our pets, and our country. 1 Corinthians 13:4-8 (NIV) states, "Love is patient, love is kind. It does not envy. It does not boast, it is not proud. It does not dishonor others, it is not self-seeking, it is not easily angered, it keeps no records of wrongs. Love does not delight in evil but rejoices with the truth. It always protects, always trusts, always hopes, always perseveres." To sum it up, love is unconditional. Therefore, it cannot be based on feelings, but rather on commitment and loyalty.

People in the military serve with honor and commitment. They selflessly fight for many reasons: to protect the people and things they love, to free those who are being oppressed, and to destroy the evil forces that want to annihilate us. They succeed because they take and follow orders; they are committed to those who fight alongside them— they do not seek their own glory. They are focused on their mission and persevere to achieve victory. They have a strong bond with each other that provides support, encouragement, and loyalty. Jesus and His disciples had the same goals and camaraderie. They got their orders from God, and they concentrated on their mission, persevered, and achieved victory. We are in a spiritual battle whether we realize it or not. Satan's goal is to take control of our thoughts so that he can control us. Therefore, it is important that we unite with other people who can support and encourage us.

As long as evil exist in the world, there will be physical wars between nations and spiritual wars between good and evil. The real commanders in charge of these battles are God and Satan. Both types of wars can cause casualties and those fighting in them can suffer mental and physical injuries. Just like a commander in the armed forces makes sure those who serve under him get encouragement and medical care if needed, God will take care of those in His army, and He will provide even more help. When we find ourselves tired of the spiritual battles this life brings, we must talk to Jesus and let Him know our deepest sorrows and fears. He knows exactly how we feel; He "is at the right hand of God and is also interceding for us" (Romans 8:34 NIV). Therefore, let's not delay in asking the Lord to help us win the battle of despair!

BATTLE PLAN: Jesus loves us; He fights for us because He left us behind when He ascended into Heaven. He promises to come back someday and get those who are His (John 14:3). In the meantime, we need to follow God's orders that are written in the Bible and seek His guidance by praying and asking for wisdom. The apostle Paul said, "I consider that our present sufferings are not worth comparing with the glory that will be revealed in us" (Romans 8:18 NIV). As in all wars, we will have seasons of suffering and pain, but also joy and healing. Thomas Fuller said that "friendships multiply joys and divide griefs." Just like military personnel support, encourage, and fight together to defeat the enemy we need to do that and surround ourselves with people who will do the same. In addition, we must trust and put our hope in God as we persevere.

BATTLE SONG: "Hope in Front of Me" by Danny Gokey

WHEN WE ARE HATED

"You will be hated by everyone because of me, but the one who stands firm to the end will be saved." —Matthew 10:22 (NIV)

The battle between good and evil has been going on ever since humans let sin enter their lives. The spirit of pride, self-love, and hate were allowed to grow in the hearts of mankind. These destructive forces have been multiplying and growing inside of people throughout the ages. Because of some people's selfish ambitions, which lead to corruption and the desire for power, wars take place. Sometimes those who fight for freedom against tyranny are betrayed by their leaders who have no loyalty to those who serve under them.

Jesus came to Earth thousands of years ago to set the captives free from the slavery of sin. However, governments still tried to control and enslave their people back then, and some still do today. The colonists in America fought for their God-given right to freedom and won their independence from England. Since then, the United States has engaged in battles to help people of other nations win their freedom from oppression and tyranny. The soldiers who fought in World War I and II were considered heroes when they returned home from the battlefield. Unfortunately, veterans who returned home from the Vietnam War were not given that honor. Some people called them horrific names and treated them poorly, even though those men and women were helping the South Vietnamese people fight the North Vietnamese who were trying to take away their freedom as an independent nation. My ex-husband fought in the Vietnam War, and people's cruelty not only broke my heart, but it also angered me.

When hate and love are compared, it is easy to see the forces that are behind each one; love allows freedom and justice, whereas hate produces oppression and corruption. The Bible says, "Repay no one evil for evil but give thought to do what is honorable in the sight of all. *If possible*, so far as it depends on you, live peaceably with all. Beloved, never avenge yourselves, but leave it to the wrath of God, for it is written, 'Vengeance is mine, I will repay, says the LORD'" (Romans 12:17-19 NKJ). This scripture has been a lifeline for me over the years. It has helped me keep my anger towards others from turning into hate.

When I have gone to God with my fury and hurt in the past, it accomplished two things: He took those feelings out of my heart because I turned them over to Him, and He dealt with the people who wronged me.

BATTLE PLAN: The apostle Paul said, "Let love be without hypocrisy. Abhor what is evil; cling to what is good" (Romans 12:9 NKJ). We are supposed to hate evil and cling to God. It is when we let Him deal with the wicked who falsely accuse and hurt us, that we are truly free from the power the enemy has over us. "It is for freedom that Christ has set us free. Stand firm, then, and do not let yourselves be burdened again by a yoke of slavery" (Galatians 5:1 NIV). Satan wants us in captivity and he will use people to bring us down. In situations like this, we must choose to surrender it all to God so we will not be overcome by evil, but will overcome evil with good (Romans 12:21).

BATTLE SONG: "Wounds" by Jordan Feliz

A TIME OF WAR, AND A TIME OF PEACE—ECCLESIASTES 3:8B

THE BATTLE IS GOD'S

"The greatness of a man's power is the measure of his surrender." —*William Booth*

Throughout the Old and New Testament of the Bible, there are so many historical events of God's faithfulness to help His people. King Jehoshaphat of Judah was told that several forces combined were on their way to attack him and his people. Instead of calling all of his military strategists together to devise a plan of defense, he went to the house of the LORD and talked to God. His prayer wasn't one of desperation, but rather of faith and trust. He reminded God of the times that He helped him and his people in battle; he stated how powerful God was and that they did not have enough power to fight the multitude. Then the king said, "but our eyes are upon You." God's answer came through a prophet named Jahaziel who said, *"Thus says the LORD to you: 'Do not be afraid nor dismayed because of this great multitude, for the battle is not yours, but God's'…you will not need to fight in this battle. Position yourselves, stand still and see the salvation* of the LORD, who is with you" (2 Chronicles 20:15,17 NKJ). The king had simply talked to God about his dilemma.

Is there a multitude of problems trying to destroy you today? Perhaps an army of anxiety has penetrated your mind. Maybe you have been fighting this enemy for so long that you have no more strength to engage the onslaught that is now approaching you. Why not do what King Jehoshaphat did? He talked to God and told Him that he couldn't win the battle without Him. He not only reminded God of what He did for him in the past, but he reminded himself of God's faithfulness. Lastly, he took his eyes off the unstoppable forces approaching him and put them on God and His ability to help fight his enemy. Is there a time when you knew that God helped you in the past? If so, remind Him of that and tell Him that you are trusting Him to help you fight the battle you are facing. Jesus once told His disciples, "With man this is impossible, but with God all things are possible" (Matthew 19:26 NIV). God loves you and wants you to live totally free from any type of oppression. Your responsibility is to ask Him for help and believe that He will do it.

BATTLE PLAN: King Jehoshaphat said to his people, "Believe in the Lord your God and you will be able to stand firm; believe His prophets, and you will succeed" (2 Chronicles 20:20 NLT). The king instructed the people to sing praises to God. As they sang, the Lord set ambushes so the enemies attacked and killed each other (2 Chronicles 22-23). God's word never changes; therefore, we must believe that He will help us. It is when we surrender our control of a situation to God and then pray and worship Him, that the battle becomes His!

BATTLE SONG: "Do It Again" by Elevation Worship

THE FIGHT FOR FREEDOM

"My most cherished possession I wish I could leave you is my faith in Jesus Christ, for with Him and nothing else you can be happy, but without Him and with all else you will never be happy." —Patrick Henry

P atrick Henry was a politician and a Founding Father of the United States. He played a major role in the American Revolution; his desire to be free from the English government's overbearing power also inspired the U.S. Bill of Rights. He truly understood that God created man to be free and that God was the supreme ruler over us. As an attorney, he also fought for religious freedom for the people, as well as against the heavy taxes and burdens England put on the colonists.

Henry realized that life was about more than just himself. Many of us realize and believe this too, but do we actually act on it? When the odds are against us or our health is failing, do we still continue to promote our beliefs or do we retreat. Patrick Henry said, "Give me Liberty or give me death." This comment inspired many to persevere and fight for freedom from tyranny. His legacy has lived on well after his death because his tenacity helped create a new world.

There are so many causes of apprehension in the world today: pandemics, politics, financial instability, and rumors of wars are but a few. It appears that many people have lost their integrity—the truth is no longer important, but rather twisted to fit people's agendas. It is much like the times of Patrick Henry's days. As Christians, we should not be surprised about the state of the world because the Bible predicted it hundreds of years ago: "But know this in the last days perilous times will come; men will be lovers of themselves, lovers of money, boasters, proud, blasphemers, unforgiving, slanderers, without self-control, brutal, despisers of good, traitors, headstrong, haughty, lovers of pleasure rather than lovers of God, having a form of godliness but denying its power And from such people turn away!" (2 Timothy 3:1-5 NKJ). It's hard to witness the corruption and immorality and not lose heart. The number of suicides is increasing as well as drug and alcohol abuse; these things are the repercussions of hopelessness.

Patrick Henry lived in dangerous yet exciting times, and he was able to accomplish amazing things because his life was surrendered to Jesus Christ. Perhaps knowing that he would spend eternity in heaven with the Lord motivated him to finish well. His faith in Jesus gave him peace and joy in a war-torn world. If we are truly children of God, we have nothing to fear because He promises us that He will be with us always. What is your most cherished possession—is it faith in Jesus? Seeing the state that the world is currently in, it is of the utmost importance to determine where we stand right now with God.

BATTLE PLAN: People in the military are trained for combat and told that they will be deployed if certain conditions arise. When the time comes, they implement all they learned and accept their assignment, whether they like it or not. Their focus is on their mission and they do their best to block everything else out of their mind so they can accomplish their objective. Likewise, a soldier in God's army must do the same thing. Wherever we are in life right now is where God has strategically placed us, for a time such as this. Ephesians 6 in the Bible talks about the armor of God that we are to put on to protect ourselves from the devil. We are called to "have nothing to do with the fruitless deeds of darkness, but rather expose them" (Ephesians 5:11 NKJ). Warriors don't hide at home afraid to confront their enemy, they hunt them down and stop them from causing destruction. Therefore, let's put on the full armor of God and go to war against the spirit of despair. With Jesus by our side, we can win the battles against fear, doubt, worry, anger, and hopelessness that attack our mind and be free at last!

BATTLE SONG: "Walk By Faith" by Jeremy Camp

GOD'S WAR

"They cried out to God in the battle. He heeded their prayer, because they put their trust in Him…for many fell dead, because the war was God's." —1 Chronicles 5:20,22 (NKJ)

There are many types of war in life: the spiritual war of good against evil; the physical war of country against country; the personal war of the spirit against the flesh; the mental war of hope and despair; and the war that is of God. Our heavenly Father allows the battles in the world, as well as the ones in our lives, so that He can fulfill His purpose. Sometimes, God allows our enemies to win against us because we have turned away from Him and He wants us to return.

The opening scripture references a battle in which the armies of Reuben, Gad, and Manasseh won because they put their trust in God and not on their own warrior skills. They prayed for God's guidance on how to proceed. In doing this, the battle was no longer theirs, it was God's. Proverbs 16:7 (NLT) states, "When people's lives please the LORD, even their enemies are at peace with them." Sometimes, peace is the result of conquering your adversary. However, there are times when God cuts down the size of the army approaching by causing confusion, and making the men attack each other (Judges 7:19-21, 1 Samuel 14:20). These war stories are not fables; they are part of the Jewish history, which is the Old Testament of the Bible. God's word and promise of yesterday is the same today and will be the same tomorrow. Are you currently losing the battle you are fighting? If so, cry out to God, and then put your trust in Him!

BATTLE PLAN: The men in the opening scripture in Chronicles were skilled warriors, but they still asked God for help in the battle. Sometimes we think we are strong enough to handle a situation and we often find ourselves exhausted and defeated. It is important for us to start praying and petitioning God to help us before we engage in a fight. Whether it is an illness, injury, relationship, or a war within our mind, once we put our trust in the Lord, we are giving Him the permission to fight for us. This concept is hard for some of us to imagine, but it is really no different than soldiers getting word that enemy forces are approaching, so they radio their commander and ask for help. Once they make the call, they have done everything they can, and they put their trust in someone who is not even there. Why do we find it so easy to put our faith in people's ability to help us, but not God's? He told us that "you do not have because you do not ask God" (James 4:2 NIV). So, we need to ask our heavenly Father for help whenever we need it. If we do not receive what we want, it may be because are motives are not right. Yet, other times He waits because He is trying to teach us something or build our faith. Sometimes God delays the answer to our prayers because He is waiting for us to repent for some sin we committed. Whatever the reason, get right with God, stay the course, and keep praying!

BATTLE SONG: "Battle Belongs" by Phil Wickham

Remembering Why We Are in a War

"He died for all, that those who live should live no longer for themselves, but for Him who died for them and rose again" --2 Corinthians 5:15 (NKJV)

Life is generally filled with good times as well as bad times. However, we can go through seasons that are filled with one battle after another. During times like this, I often find myself complaining to God about my circumstances. When I start grumbling, I know I need to spend more time with Him by reading my Bible and my devotionals. God is so faithful; He always leads me somewhere in His word that reminds me that I surrendered my life to Him, He is fighting alongside me, and will provide what I need to survive the battle. It is through the turbulent times in our lives that we look for reassurance that things will be okay. Sometimes, we find hope through people who have survived the same situation that we are facing.

It was during the times when the enemies' torpedoes almost overpowered me, that God was using me as a vessel to bring people to Him. Some people watched as I kept afloat through the stormy seas of cancer, others saw forgiveness when ominous winds of abuse hit me, while some observed the unstable clouds of my finances and the blessings that followed. Witnessing God's faithfulness to get me through and bring healing was the catalyst for many people to turn their lives over to Him. They finally realized that I was telling the truth when I said that I was not a strong person, but that "I can do all things through Christ who strengthens me" (Philippians 4:13 NKJ). The power of Christ is in us, but we must believe we have it, and we also need to use it.

Christian apologist G. K. Chesterton once said, "The true soldier fights not because he hates what is in front of him, but because he loves what is behind him." Many Americans joined the armed forces after the 9/11 terrorist attack on the United States. They wanted to make sure that nobody would hurt the people they loved again. The Christian soldier fights not because they love their life, but because they love others and want to see them safely in heaven when they die, rather than suffering in hell. Who or what are you currently living for?

BATTLE PLAN: The world is getting crazier every day, and at the time of this writing, there is fighting in Ukraine and rumors of potential war with other nations. Many people are unsure of where they will spend eternity, therefore, as soldiers for Christ we need to be engaged in the battle because nobody knows the day or time that Jesus will return for us. If you are not a Christian, realize that you have a heavenly Father that wants to spend eternity with you, and He is waiting for you to let Him into your life. C. S. Lewis once said, "Believe in God like you believe in the sunrise. Not because you can see it, but because you can see all it touches." Open your eyes and look for the light of Jesus shining in the life of those around you; they will lead you through the war to victory!

BATTLE SONG: "The Light in Me" by Brandon Heath

FIGHTING FOR YOUR LIFE

"Desire that your life count for something great! Long for your life to have eternal significance. Want this! Don't coast through life without a passion." —John Piper

There are many reasons why people lose their zeal in life: loss of a job, an injury, illness, betrayal, and grief are but a few. Shattered dreams can be devastating; however, God can make beauty out of ashes, and He promises to work things together for good for those who love Him (Romans 8:28 KJV). Sometimes it is our choice to make the change in our life; maybe we decide to retire from our job or our service in the military and retirement is not what we imagined it would be like. We don't know what to do with all the time we now have. Being sedentary or isolated opens the door for the enemy to attack. There is an idiom that says: an *idle mind is the devil's playground*. When our minds are empty, he can fill them with hopelessness and fear, which causes anxiety and depression. God tells us in His word: "Do not be overcome by evil but overcome evil with good" (Romans 12:21 NIV). Therefore, we need to fight our desires to just give up; instead, we need to put on our armor and go to war against the enemy.

God has a plan for this new season of our lives, and our training requires us to seek His guidance daily. As we read His word and pray, He not only encourages us, but He can give us glimpses of our future. He may put a desire in our heart to pursue a new career, or to remind us of a talent we were born with, which is usually something that we enjoy doing and brings us happiness. I know that God does this because he did this for me. I have actually had several professions: legal secretary, plan administrator (for a financial institution), surgical technologist, clinical instructor, teacher, missionary, tutor, and author. I chose to leave these positions because God would either change my life's circumstances or He would put a desire in my heart to do something new. The catalysts that caused me to leave jobs were a bad blizzard, motherhood, divorce, a desire to be in the medical field, the death of my second husband, the desire to be a missionary, and my love for teaching and writing. I went back to school several times for different degrees and had to pass tests to be licensed for a couple of jobs. Each time I decided to make a change, the enemy would attack and bombard my mind with doubt, confusion, fear, and insecurity. Sometimes he even sent people to discourage me! The secret to prevailing over the devil's attacks was to seek God's word and guidance daily, believe what I read, and then trust God to get me through, and He did! God can do this for you too, but you have to commit to Him and His plan for your life. Satan offers death, God offers life—choose life!!!

BATTLE PLAN: God designed Earth to have four seasons and each one serves its own special purpose. When one ends, another one automatically begins, which is a reminder that change is needed and it is a good thing. God created us in a similar fashion, there are times when we are productive and accomplish our mission and other times when find ourselves on "inactive duty" so that we can rest and be trained to accomplish something different. Both stages are productive in their own way and contribute to the big scheme of things. Author Charles Dickens once said. "Nature gives to every time and season some beauties of its own." Change is hard, but everything in life changes, therefore, we must be able to adapt to change. The great thing about God is that He never changes, and He will be with us as we adapt to the conditions of the new season we have entered. When we let Him guide our life, the journey can be challenging but so rewarding.

BATTLE SONG: "Seasons" by Hillsong Worship

PEACE INSTEAD OF FEAR

"Peace I leave with you, My peace I give to you; not as the world gives do I give to you. Let not your heart be troubled, neither let it be afraid" —John 14:27 (NKJV)

One of the world's definitions of peace is tranquility; it's being free from war, anxiety, worry, and hardship. This definition is skewed because the world's peace is only temporary. Even if there is peace between nations, it can change at any time. The same applies to our personal life; we can feel safe and secure in our country, but are our finances, health, and future assured? I believe the answer to that question is no because nothing is guaranteed in life. That is why Jesus said that His peace is not like the peace the world offers—His is unshakeable.

Isaiah 26:3 (NKJV) states, "You (God) will keep him in perfect peace whose mind is stayed on You, because he trusts in You." Worldly peace involves us working hard to secure our future, eating healthy, and making good choices. God wants us to work, eat well, and make wise decisions too, however, even if we do those things, there are always situations that arise that are out of our control. I ate healthy and exercised daily, yet I was still diagnosed with cancer twice. Fortunately, God had built my faith and trust in Him over the years, and I was able to have peace even though my future was uncertain. My trust was not in my ability or my doctors, but rather in my heavenly Father's promises. Jesus said, "If you can believe, all things are possible to him who believes" Mark 9:23 (NKJV). By choosing to believe, I was set free from fear, worry, and the stress of my disease. I have been cancer free for ten years now and God came through for me in every area of my life. Asking Him to guide me to the right doctors, to provide for me financially, and to help me get through everything was the best thing I could have done. Do you believe that God has the ability to do everything?

When God made the moon (Gen 1:14-18), He orchestrated its rotation around Earth with gravity that pulls the ocean toward or away from the moon; this is how the tides work. God said, "Will you not tremble at My presence, who have placed the sand as the bound of the sea, by a perpetual decree, that it cannot pass beyond it" (Jerimiah 5:22 NKJV)? If God can synchronize the heavens and the earth, He is more than capable of coordinating the events in our lives. The only thing that stops Him from doing this is us.

BATTLE PLAN: We need to build faith in God's promises, and we must also learn to ask Him to intervene in our lives. The best time to get rooted in God's word is when life is going well for us. Then, when the storm appears out of nowhere and our future is uncertain, we know the promises God made to us and we can claim them and believe He will come through for us.

The enemy of your soul will do everything he can to keep you from reading the bible, so that you will have doubt in times of adversity. One of my favorite scriptures from the Bible is: "Be anxious for nothing, but in everything by prayer and supplication, with thanksgiving, let your requests be made known to God; and the peace of God, which surpasses all understanding, will guard your hearts and minds through Christ Jesus" Philippians 4:6-7 NKJV). The best soldier has a battle strategy before the fight begins. Therefore, being armed with scripture will keep our minds in peace through times of uncertainty.

BATTLE SONG: "You Are I Am" by MercyMe

PEACE IN THE PRESENCE OF ENEMIES

"Most people are about as happy as they make their mind up to be." —Abraham Lincoln

There is a Christian saying that states, "It is a choice to rejoice." No matter how bad our situation is we can always find something to be thankful for. King Saul in the Old Testament of the Bible attempted to kill David over a dozen times. Although David was anointed by God to be king when he was a shepherd boy, he was not trying to take the throne from Saul. In fact, David respected and served Saul until Saul set out to kill him.

Psalm 23, written by David, is a good example of how a person can choose to have peace and joy in a dire situation. In verse 4 of the Psalm, David is walking through "the valley of the shadow of death." However, he reminds himself that God is with him, and he puts his faith in God's ability to protect him. Once David surrendered his fear to God, his mind was free to focus on other things, so he chose to concentrate on all the times God had helped him in the past.

Verse 5 of Psalm 23 ends with "my cup overflows" and verse 6 begins with "Surely your goodness and love will follow me all the days of my life." Perspective of a situation is so important. When we look at the cup of life as half empty we have a pessimistic attitude, but when we view our cup as half full, our thoughts are optimistic. Preacher Jonathan Edwards once said, "Life is a journey toward heaven. Why should we labor for anything else, but that which is our proper end and true happiness?" David shared this same view because he ended Psalm twenty-three with these words: "And I will dwell in the house of the LORD forever." He realized that his time on Earth was limited, and that God would get him through his time here. This allowed him to have peace in the presence of his enemies. What do you believe?

BATTLE PLAN: The ordinary person doesn't really think about death until they get old or are diagnosed with a deadly disease. Whereas the soldier, police officer, fireman, or missionary usually thinks about death before venturing into that profession. This, however, does not mean that they are happy with the possibility of death, but they are aware of the possibility and make the choice to still move forward. I believe that David was confident in God's ability not his own ability and that is why his attitude was upbeat. President Abraham Lincoln's words had some truth to them; although we cannot prevent all bad things from happening, we can choose like David to find good in everything.

BATTLE SONG: "Goodness, Love and Mercy" by Chris Tomlin

HOLDING YOUR PEACE

"The LORD will fight for you, and you shall hold your peace." —Exodus 14:14 (NKJ)

We don't hear the phrase "hold your peace" much these days. However, if you have attended a wedding recently you may have heard this phrase during the ceremony: "Should anyone present know of any reason that this couple should not be joined in holy matrimony, speak now or forever hold your peace." This is stating that if you don't speak up now, do not speak later about the situation even if it is upsetting you.

Exodus 14 in the Bible is about the Israelites crossing the Red Sea when the Egyptians were chasing them. The people came to a place where they were trapped and had no way to move forward. "Do not be afraid. Stand still and see the salvation of the LORD, which He will accomplish for you today," said Moses (Exodus 14:13 (NKJ). He was reassuring the people that they should trust God, be quiet, and accept what was happening. As most of us know, God parted the Red Sea and they walked on the ocean floor, with walls of water on each side, to the land on the other side of the sea. The Egyptians followed, but God allowed the seawalls to cave in and drown Pharoah and his soldiers.

Although we may not be currently running for our lives from foreign enemies, we often find ourselves in a place where it is impossible to move forward. Moses sought God when he was trapped and asked for His help—that is what we must do also. Accepting our dilemma and waiting silently can be difficult, as well as scary. We don't have to be trapped by a physical enemy; it can be the adversary of regret, fear, depression, or hopelessness. Since God promises that He will "never leave you nor forsake you" (Hebrews 13:5 NKJ), we need to put our trust in Him to part the sea of despair that is blocking our escape.

BATTLE PLAN: As you can see from the history in the Bible, God likes to perform miracles and rescue His people in miraculous ways: raising Lazarus from the dead (John 11:38-44); feeding five thousand plus people with five loaves of bread and two fish (Matthew 14:13-21); and orchestrating a poor Jewish girl, named Ester, to become the queen of Persia and save the Jewish nation from annihilation. It was through these circumstances that people saw that God existed, which built their trust and faith in Him. Therefore, when there are no human resources available to help us when we are trapped, it just might be because God wants to reveal His existence through our lives. All we have to do is surrender our situation to Him, hold our peace, and let Him fight for us!

BATTLE SONG: "Faith" by Jordan Feliz

FINDING PEACE

"Nobody can bring you peace but yourself." —*Ralph Waldo Emerson*

According to *Psychology Today* the average person makes 35,000 decisions per day! When I read that I thought...*this can't be true.* I did research and found that there are many websites that say the same thing. Everything we do or don't do during the day, is choice that we have to make. Even if a situation is out of our control and a choice isn't required, we still have to choose how we will react to the circumstance. Decision-making can be practical, emotional, or experiential; sometimes we don't know how to approach a situation, so we ignore it and hope that it solves itself. However, as we wait, it still weighs heavy on our hearts and minds.

Mahatma Gandhi said something similar to Emerson but elaborated on it: "Each one has to find peace from within. And peace to be real must be unaffected by outside circumstances." That can be a hard goal for us to achieve on our own; thank God we have a great role model—Jesus! No matter what was happening to Him, He was calm, and He had peace. He came to Earth to fulfill a purpose and He was focused on His mission, so His decisions were all centered around that one goal. Instead of worrying over things that got in His way, He made sure that He spent time daily seeking His Father's guidance and praying. This did not consist of a quick prayer in between meetings with His disciples. He specifically went away from people so He would not be disturbed. If we are having difficulty finding peace, we need to ask ourselves these questions: How often do I spend uninterrupted time with God? When I do, am I doing all the talking and listing things I want Him to do for me, or am I asking God how He wants me to precede and trusting that He will work things out for my good?

BATTLE PLAN: The prophet Isaiah was called by God to bring a warning message to the Jewish people: repent of your evil ways and turn back to God. If they didn't, God would punish them. I imagine that Isaiah was not popular amongst the people because of the message he was called to deliver. Isaiah composed a song that is in the Old Testament of the Bible (in Isaiah 26 NKJ). Verse 3-4 states: "You will keep him in perfect peace, whose mind is stayed on You, because he trusts in You. Trust in the Lord forever for in Yah, the Lord, is everlasting strength." I am assuming that Isaiah was able to complete his mission because this is how he dealt with the decisions he had to make. So, this is how we can have peace during our times of turmoil—keep our mind on God, trust in Him, and He will give us strength. When I think about the quotes from Emerson and Gandhi, I understand what they meant; it is up to us to choose peace in chaos. Through the daily decision to trust God and stay focused on His plan for our lives, we can let go of the stress, anxiety, and fear that comes with difficult choices because we are taking the practical, emotional, and experiential thinking out of the equation—that's what Jesus did! When we trade in our ways for God's ways, He promises to give us peace through the storms because our mind is on Him and His ability. Out of the 35,000 daily decisions we have to make, this one will be the best one we could ever make!

BATTLE SONG: "Peace" by Danny Gokey

AFTERWORD

Psalm 91 (NKJV) has been my battle scripture, especially when I was abroad on the mission field. God's words in the verses below came alive for me and they can for you, too!

1. He who dwells in the secret place of the Most High shall abide under the shadow of the Almighty.
2. I will say of the LORD, "He is my refuge and my fortress; My God, in Him I will trust."
3. Surely He shall deliver you from the snare of the fowler and for the perilous pestilence.
4. He shall cover you with His feathers, and under His wings you shall take refuge; His truth shall be your shield and buckler.
5. You shall not be afraid of the terror by night, nor of the arrow that flies by day.
6. Nor of the pestilence that walks in darkness, nor of the destruction that lays waste at noonday.
7. A thousand may fall at your side, and ten thousand at your right hand; but it shall not come near you.
8. Only with your eyes shall you look and see the reward of the wicked.

9. Because you have made the LORD, who is my refuge, even the Most High, your dwelling place.
10. No evil shall befall you, nor shall any plague come near your dwelling place.
11. For He shall give His angels charge over you, to keep you in all your ways.
12. In their hands they shall bear you up, lest you dash your foot against a stone.
13. You shall tread upon the lion and the cobra, the young lion and the serpent you shall trample underfoot.
14. Because he has set his love upon Me, therefore, I will deliver him; I will set him on high, because he has known My name.
15. He shall call upon Me, and I will answer him; I will be with him in trouble; I will deliver him and honor him.
16. With long life I will satisfy him, and show him My Salvation.

I pray that out of his glorious riches He may strengthen you with power through His spirit in your inner being so that Christ may dwell in your heart through faith. And I pray that you, being rooted and established in love, may have power, together with all the Lord's holy people, to grasp how wide and long and high and deep is the love of Christ, and to know this love that surpasses knowledge—that you may be filled to the measure of all the fullness of God. To Him who is able to do immeasurably more than all we ask or imagine, according to His power that is at work within us, to Him be the glory in the church and in Christ Jesus throughout all generations, forever and ever! Amen (Ephesians 3:16-21).

God Bless You!
Deb

Printed in the USA
CPSIA information can be obtained
at www.ICGtesting.com
LVHW021226191023
761201LV00006B/55